STEVEN J. CRAIG

ITALY

TRAVEL & ADVENTURES

ROME, VENICE,
THE CINQUE TERRE
AND NEARBY VILLAGES

'Lol, your writing style is hilarious and entertaining while informing and educating. I love it. It's a good read.'

B. Korson
Denver, CO

"The most comprehensive guidebook on Italy I have read. A must for both first-time and experienced travelers."

Robert Nelson
Brier, Washington

Contents   Page

Pictures by Steven Craig unless otherwise noted. Lodging pictures provided and used with permission.

Cover design by JD Smith.

Chapter 1
Advance Planning
Ciao (Chow)
Hello/Goodbye

You have your dates scheduled for your vacation. You have a dog and house sitter. You are ready to plan and reserve your air, lodging and other events. What do you do now?

Below are some questions to answer in advance:

- ❖ Do your homework. What are the issues that one needs to know?
- ❖ What do I need to do to best plan my absence from home? What are the security issues I need to consider?
- ❖ What is the best, simple way to record my travel plans?
- ❖ Do I need to bring my laptop or tablet?
- ❖ How much money do I plan to spend on lodging and food?
- ❖ Where do I plan on visiting? Have I researched the area?
- ❖ What time of year is the best time to visit? What festivals do I want to attend?
- ❖ How do I make reservations for popular tourist sites?
- ❖ How many days will I spend at each location?
- ❖ How will I get around? Taxi, train, subway, or rental car? What are the benefits?
- ❖ What is my medical coverage outside of my home country and am I fully covered?
- ❖ How will I communicate back home? Does my cell phone service provider have a special rate for out of the country?
- ❖ How will I pay for lodging and food? Do all places take credit cards?

- ❖ What security measures do I need to be aware of while traveling?
- ❖ Where can I obtain air, food and lodging recommendations?
- ❖ What side trips do I plan on taking? What special events or festivals do I want to attend?
- ❖ What language skills do I need to know?
- ❖ What Italian translator programs can assist me in communicating in Italy?
- ❖ Do I need to notify my credit card company and bank in advance?
- ❖ What is the best way to exchange my money to Euros?
- ❖ How do I pack? What do I need to pack and for how many days? How will I wash and dry my clothes?

Research

The first step is to research where you want to go. What events, sites, cities or villages do you want to visit? The Internet is a vast wealth of information; I utilize TripAdvisor or Booking.com for much of my research. Talk to friends who have been to Italy, and read further in this book for my recommendations. Base your decisions on what you want, and the impartial recommendations of others who have no financial interest. See Tab B for a listing of recommended lodgings in the cities mentioned in this book; I received no monetary compensation for these recommendations.

Also note that there are dozens of festivals held each year throughout all parts of Italy. They are quite enjoyable and range from various forms of music to different types of food or wine. See Tab C for a small listing of festivals held each year.

Creating a List

When planning my trip, I create a list utilizing MS Excel showing the status of my air, lodging, and supplies. With this planning list, I color code for status tracking purposes - green means everything is a go; yellow means the reservation is pending a final agreement with the lodging facility or the tour group. Once the list is final, I create a copy that goes to myself and a relative in case of an emergency while on vacation. Additionally, I will save the list in my email file so I can access it anywhere that has computer access.

Air

Research the airline ticket prices. There are some special fares out there. I utilize TripAdvisor using their trip alerts for some special rates. We have also used airline points to get even better deals. Check your credit card to see if they offer airline points, if not, then I would research online for some special deals. Just be sure to check their annual fees and interest rate.

> Check out 'Scott's Cheap Flights' for last-minute airline deals. List your mobile phone number and Internet email address to receive special airfare information as it becomes available. The site has a free version plus a fee service, but costs are minimal for the potential to save hundreds.
>
> https://scottscheapflights.com

Connecting Flights

When making air reservations, most flights to Italy have connections before arriving, often in Germany or London. I highly recommend checking the time length between flights. I can tell you personally that it is not a great experience for 50+year old folks to go running from one terminal to the next because there is only a 40-minute connection between flights. We found out the hard way that often terminals in international airports can be practically a mile away from each other. After landing in London, we experienced this 'event' running like wild dogs chasing sheep, just to arrive in the nick of time to board our flight; I can guarantee you, that is a picture many people would just as soon forget! Unfortunately, our luggage did not arrive at our destination, and we were forced to wear the same clothes for another day until it finally arrived.

Checking Baggage

Some people have problems with checked baggage; we have had very few issues. But I recommend that you only check items you can afford to lose. For carry-on bags, we bring our laptop or tablets, makeup (not me), and pharmaceutical drugs. For those bags you do check, I recommend you put your name, address and contact information inside the bag should the name tag get ripped off while in transit.

Entertainment on Flights

It's a long flight, accept it, embrace it. I recommend you bring a couple of paperbacks, earplugs, your favorite magazines and a sleep mask. Most airlines have in-flight entertainment, and I will readily pay the nominal fee to watch a mindless movie to pass the time away. The ear plugs are worth a million bucks when sitting close to a jabbering person or noisy children. On the flip side, I have found some very fascinating people while on long flights. Listening to their stories will help the time fly.

Airline Boarding Tickets

Printing your boarding tickets at home is an easy and efficient way to speed up the check-in process at airports. But what if it is not recognized at the TSA checkpoint? This issue happened to us, with the friendly TSA agent stating that sometimes the printer at home will not align properly. You need to conduct the printer test at home before printing the ticket to ensure your cartridge is installed correctly. My preference is to make sure I can get through the TSA line without any possible interruptions. I print my boarding pass at the airport.

I would also recommend registering for the TSA Pre-Check program where you can skip the long security lines at the airport. At the time of this book printing, the program cost was $85 for five years and allows you to go through the lines, where you don't need to remove your shoes, laptop, liquids, belts and light jackets. You simply log-on to register, then proceed to one of the designated centers with your identification. Recommendation: Review the listed locations and if a small town is nearby, register for that office. We found one that was of equal distance to Seattle and Portland and we were the only customers there! They very friendly and efficient. In fact, I think they were sad to see us go.

Bank Notifications and Credit Cards

Once you have your dates figured out, then notify your bank and any credit cards you may be using overseas. There is nothing worse than having a snooty Italian waiter tell you in a rather loud voice that "sir, your credit card is no good!" I still remember that moment ten years ago when communicating back to my home state was difficult, at best, during that period to resolve this situation. When I asked the next day why the card was declined, the company replied because it had been used in Italy. I won't make that mistake again.

Regarding credit card use I always take three credit cards and one debit card. A debit card is invaluable for obtaining quick cash from the many ATMs located nationwide. Also, check to see if your credit card has an international transaction fee. Upon my return, I found I had spent over $100 on such fees. Some credit card companies waive this fee; check first before you leave. As a final step, I take pictures of my credit cards, front and back, should they 'disappear.' I then scan the photos into an email to myself with password protection. Getting stuck in Italy without a credit card can be most unpleasant.

Lodging

When planning, I complete a lodging list showing name, confirmation numbers, dates, locations, and contact phone numbers. Making reservations these days is a simple matter, but I prefer to check reviews before I reserve a room. On many occasions, I have booked through Booking.com to add an extra security measure. If staying in a hotel, I record the reservation number and keep a copy of the e-mail. With some of the smaller places you will need to pay cash; some take credit cards, some will ask that you wire the payment which your bank will assist you in. Wire payments from your credit union may be somewhat difficult or impossible; I prefer to reserve with a credit card whenever possible. Whatever the method of payment, review the lodging to make certain they are reputable. Scams exist, but careful diligence on your part should ensure a secure trip. Knock on wood, to date, I have never been ripped-off by any vendor in Italy. Again, reading reviews from reputable sites should ensure a safe and secure trip.

Another issue you may need to address is the type of bed you desire. The European standards are different. You will find hotels will offer different bed sizes: Single, Double, Triple and sometimes Quad. A single bed, normally, has one twin-size bed; a double may have two twin beds, either separate or pushed together to make one bed or a double bed. A triple has some mixture of the two possibilities above and a quad also has some combination of singles and doubles. Queen size beds, which are common in the United States, are rare in Europe. The closest to it is two twin beds pushed together, as mentioned above.

On one of our trips, we decided to stay at a variety of lodging establishments. On this two-month vacation, we stayed at an apartment, a bed & breakfast, a working farm (called an agriturismo), and a hotel. The hotel had a natural hot springs pool that was fantastic; the apartment was in a remote region of Italy (and I mean remote) that also had a private museum next door, and the bed and breakfast lodging was situated in a beautiful country setting overlooking the scenic valley. Another type of lodging is that of an affittacamere (ahf-feet-ah-KAH-meh-reh), which are rooms to rent. These are popular in those communities that may not have the hotel capacity to handle a significant influx of tourists, such as the villages of the Cinque Terre.

The point here is to experience Italy to the fullest by staying in various lodging establishments, in both large cities and small villages. I rely heavily on TripAdvisor and Booking.com for reliable, impartial recommendations. These websites can also give you an idea of the costs; the apartment was less than $100 per night while the hotel with the hot springs was near $300 per night. Both were well worth the money. Do your research, check reliable sources, and you should not have any problems.

Language

What level of Italian language skill will you need to know? I would recommend a basic knowledge of routine tourist terms, such as those related to restaurants, lodging and asking directions. For the life of me, I have taken numerous language lessons with no success; there are some excellent programs out there, but sometimes I think they are simply beyond me. I concentrate on knowing what food I am ordering, how to ask for the check, how to ask directions and some other terms relating to basic conversation.

On an elementary level, you can get by with very little understanding of Italian. You will find that in the larger cities, most of the businesses associated with tourism have employees who speak excellent English. In the smaller, remote parts of Italy, you'll be lucky to find one who speaks English. I have found that when I don't know the correct Italian word, I point or gesture and smile.

Probably the best solution, without investing hundreds of hours in learning a new language, is to download an app that can translate English to Italian and vice versa; both in written form and as audio. I have tried the Google Translate app and found it very easy to use; not to mention helping to reduce the number of hand signals I use to convey my message.

The bottom line: don't let Italian language skills, or lack of, delay your trip. Just do it with the right attitude, and you will do fine.

Like the guy at the food stand who sold me a hamburger. I said hamburger, he says, no it is HumBURgur....and I reply that is what I said. As I stated before, Italians admire when you try, but sometimes you can see their eyebrows crinkle up when you speak. That part I love. "Let's see them cringe today while I butcher their language!" I give up. I can't speak Italian and never will. Try saying Alba, a city in Italy. I stated All-ba and am told it is Al-ba. This is from a guy who lived in El-ma, whose wife came from El-be, I used to live near Ad-na, and Italy has an island called El-be! Between the different ways you say A or E in English or Italian, it is easy to get confused.

Guided Tours

There are many advantages to selecting a guided tour. Planning on your part is very minimal; the tour guide knows the area and can provide more detailed explanation of the villages and people, and the mode of travel is already determined. There are some excellent travel agencies such as AAA (http://www.com), Rick Steves (https://www.ricksteves.com/), and other vendors that can take the hassles and headaches out of planning such a trip. Whether you pick one of these agencies or choose another, you must also review to research complaints and reviews and then make a judgment call on which tour group you would feel the most comfortable with. The price should also be considered. A red flag should be apparent when selecting a company that has not been in existence very long with very few reviews. No matter what the advertised price, remember the adage *'if it sounds too good to be true, it is.'* Every year there are stories of people who have signed up for tours only to have their money disappear. Good research on your part should help reduce the odds of this happening to you.

For a list of recommended tours, visit chapter 3 of this book.

Self-Guided Tours

Organizing and running your very own self-guided tour is an excellent way to keep costs down versus following a tour group with a set schedule. But research is key to proper planning; if you are unwilling or unable to plan a trip, then a guided tour may be your best option. Where do you want to go? If you know, then a little research on the history of the desired location can assist you with understanding more of the people and the villages of the region. If you are not sure, then conducting research based on what you are looking for will guide you toward what you desire to visit. Whether your interests are in history, beauty, the architecture, the people, the wine, or the food, Italy has everything to satisfy your desires.

How much do you want to spend? Self-guided trips for yourself can be less expensive, but you may miss out on the historical aspects of the area if you have not done any research yourself. A reasonable priced resource for understanding the local area is the website 'toursbylocal.com.' I've had excellent results with the tours I have signed up through this Internet site.

Advance travel planning is a must to obtain the best deals on airlines and lodging. I usually plan at least nine months out to ensure I get the best deals and the accommodations I want. Those places on the "most recommended" sites, such as TripAdvisor or Booking.com, are also the ones that fill up fast.

At one venue, we were attending the local annual potato festival (okay, we were bored that day) where there was music and plenty of food. The festival is held annually in a small village of fewer than 500 people, which is about right for what we enjoy. Upon leaving the festival the local police had put up road signs that I didn't understand. I turned left in my rental car at which time the police began yelling and pointedly asking me, "What? You can't read Italian!" At least I think that is what they were saying. As soon as I started speaking, in terrible Italian, the police officer smiled and turned to his partners and said something about "Americanos." One polite police officer then stepped up and gave me directions on how to get out of there, in equally bad English. We left and then spent two hours lost, driving around the countryside. At least it was a pretty drive.

Festivals, Festivals, Festivals

Italy abounds with food, wine, and music festivals. Sometimes I will tie parts of my trip to specific festivals depending on the dates and locations. These festivals can be somewhat crowded with other tourists, but are still enjoyable with parades, exhibits, games, and wine or food tastings. See Tab C for a partial listing of festivals.

Did you know Italians celebrate Valentine's Day? I didn't. A few years back, I visited a village near Milan with my wife. Immediately on our arrival, my wife became sick with the flu. Leaving the wife alone to find a decent restaurant, I found one only a block away. Arriving early (as is typical for Americans) I was soon surrounded by other Italian couples as they came to eat dinner. Only when I noticed how dressed up they were, did I realize that Italians celebrate Valentine's Day as well as Americans. Thinking back, I can only smile at how pathetic I looked, eating dinner by myself, in the corner of the restaurant.

Medical
Check with your insurance representative regarding any medical emergencies that could occur in Italy. Italy has an impressive medical program however you need to be familiar with what is covered by your company. Knowing in advance could save you much aggravation down the road; don't take the position that nothing will happen.

From Medicare.gov: "Because Medicare has limited coverage of health care services outside the U.S., you may choose to buy a travel insurance policy to get more coverage. An insurance agent or travel agent can give you more information about buying travel insurance. Travel insurance doesn't necessarily include health insurance, so it's important to read the conditions or restrictions carefully."

Traveling in Italy

Before arriving in Italy, you should reserve train and rental car services in advance from a reputable agency, although for short train trips there is no need as you can purchase on-site. There are many advantages and disadvantages of utilizing the various modes of traveling in Italy. See the next chapter for some recommendations.

Rental Cars

My first comment: Are you crazy? I have done it three times, and each time I wondered what the heck was I thinking! However, if you want to visit the remote and beautiful small villages, notably those in Tuscany, then renting a car may be your best, and only bet. Utilizing Google

Maps for GPS or other GPS tools is a must to assist you on where you want to go. As an example, there is nothing worse, than leaving Asti for a short trip to the Turin airport, and then arrive three hours later...back in Asti. That was a long day. As with renting a car, you will find that stop lights are mere suggestions along with freeway speeds. And those white stripes on the highway? I have no idea what they mean because no one drives within the lanes.

Along these same lines, consider purchasing an international driver's license; costs are reasonable and can be purchased at AAA. While I have never been asked to show proof, the cost is minimal compared to the chance of a vacation being derailed.

My most frustrating driving experiences involve renting a car from a company located in a major metropolitan area where you can easily get lost just trying to get out of the city. I have found it is easier to simply take a train to a smaller community, and rent the car from that location. Believe me, leaving and returning to the rental car agency in a medium size town with fewer streets is a whole lot less stressful.

We are lost for 2 to 3 hours trying to find our next lodging in a remote part of Italy, Piedmont Region. I narrow it down to one area, and we find this dirt road that is crossing over different hills in the remote countryside. I finally stop at a bed and breakfast that looks promising and asks the owner if we have the right address. *"No, we are not the one. You are looking for the one that is 200 meters down the road. We have been watching for you"*. What? They have a neighborhood watch looking for two lost Americanos? Apparently so.

Train

I am impressed with train travel in Italy. Unlike train travel in the United States where trains are often late, train travel in Europe is extremely punctual to the point that if you are a minute late, the train has left. The tickets are easy to purchase from one of their machines and directions are also easy to understand. Traveling throughout Italy via train is a smart way to go. You can get to Milan, Venice, Turin, Cinque Terre and many other touristy points of destination. It does restrict you to a certain degree, in some highly desired areas such as Tuscany, but often local tour companies or town buses can be utilized.

The trains themselves range from quite comfortable and modern, to basic rail cars with graffiti spray written on the side. But I have always found train travel to be safe. If you are going to Venice or Milan from Rome, you need to experience one of the bullet trains. These trains can get up to speeds over 200 mph and get you to your destination quite quickly.

Money

Once I arrive in Italy, the first stop I make is to the airport ATM. Here money can be obtained in euros. The charges are reasonable, and that is how I pay for most of the trip when credit cards are not accepted. Keep in mind that some places don't accept credit cards and will require cash. Some establishments will require a wire transfer. I generally will reserve somewhere else as I am somewhat leery of these types of transactions. I try to keep at least 200 euro in my wallet especially when traveling the countryside. ATMs, while abundant in cities, can be a challenge to find in the smaller villages.

Security

In some ways, Italy is safer than the United States when talking about personal security and major crime. But when it comes to pickpockets, they can excel. Just be aware of your surroundings, notably around major train stations or subways. I always use a money belt to ensure my money and passport are safe. This item I purchase from my local AAA travel store or online stores such as travel expert RickSteves.com.

I had mentioned earlier about taking photocopies of your credit cards should they be stolen or misplaced. Also make copies of your passport, driver's license and anything else of value. Keep these copies in a safe place that you can access immediately should you need to. Storing a copy in a password protected email to yourself isn't a bad idea either. That way even if your tablet or smartphone is stolen, you can still access the information.

Electric Converters

Italy utilizes 220 volts versus 110 volts in the United States.   Not only are the voltages different, but so are the sockets themselves. Visitors using laptops, cell phones, battery chargers and hair dryers need to procure an electrical converter. I recommend purchasing a converter in advance, particularly if you are traveling throughout Italy where a converter may not be available for sale. Many electrical retail outlets should have them.   Don't even think about using an electrical device without a converter. There is nothing more embarrassing than blowing out a section of a hotel's electrical grid because you thought that if the hair dryer fits into the plugin, then it must work without any issues. Believe me; there are issues. I was just glad we weren't homeless after that 'incident.'

Calling Home

When I first visited Italy over twelve years ago, I needed to make an emergency phone call to my wife. Imagine my frustration at trying to find enough coins for the phone booth in a remote section of Italy. Nowadays, cell phone companies have simplified the process along with providing cheaper service. Contact your local service provider to inquire about what is available and how much. Some companies have a temporary service you can purchase where you are only charged for what you use. You may also want to consider Skype as an alternative, inexpensive way to call home.

Packing

A word of warning: You buy it; you carry it. You must realize that many villages and cities in Italy are located up the hill or atop a mountain; this was for better protection from enemy invaders during early times. Walking up some very steep streets is tough enough. Walking with more than one piece of heavy luggage will most definitely take a toll on you. I learned that the hard way and hopefully, you will heed my advice. Carrying a 55 lb backpack up the steep streets of Riomaggiore, in the rain, was a memory I would just as soon forget. Although I will admit, there is a certain amount of entertainment watching three young women pulling their large luggage pieces up a very steep cobblestone street in Bellagio. You know they just had to have everything that was in their bags when they were initially packing. I wonder if they still felt that way when they finally arrived at their hilltop hotel.

In the past, I tried packing so I only had to do laundry once a week, which resulted in some rather heavy bags. Now I pack for three days, and unless I have excessively perspired, (climbing the hills of Italy), I will usually wear my clothes for two days. Often you can hand wash your clothes in a sink and let dry for the day. When packing, prioritize what you want versus what you need. Laundromats are another resource but can be rather expensive. I prefer to save my money and spend it on important things...like pasta, pesto, pizza, and wine.

'Rambling stuff' about Italy....Most stores close on Sunday, but many restaurants are open. Restaurants routinely close around 2 pm and reopen at 7 or 8 pm. Menus include various 'courses' of dinner (Antipasto, first, second, dessert, coffee or grappa). Most lodging includes a toilet, sink, and bidet. A lot of the public toilets are disgusting, but restaurant and snack bar restrooms are decent. As mentioned previously, churches are beautiful buildings although the first time you see a 'relic' below the alter it can be somewhat unsettling. 'Relics' are simply a person who was important to the church, so they put all or a portion of the deceased, inside a glass case, usually below the altar. Motorcyclists are insane, driving between cars on busy highways or cutting corners; I don't understand why they don't get killed. Car, motorcycle, and bike rallies occur every weekend, and you need to keep alert. On one visit, there was a VW rally with about 60 cars that drove by (including the 'Herbies 53). In Montepulciano, we went by a Fiat rally with about 150 cars, and later, passed a motorcycle rally with about a hundred bikes near Bagno Vignoni.

Italia! Magazine

I love this magazine! I have been a subscriber for over seven years, and I look forward to a new edition each month. The articles are one to three pages each, with some outstanding color pictures on almost every page. The magazine includes history, culture, traditions, festivals, language lessons, and food recipes. The latter comes with bright and beautiful pictures of the food that makes you want to go to the local food market and try your hand at making these delicious Italian dishes. This magazine is a great resource to read before taking your trip of a lifetime. You can find this magazine on sale at most bookstores along with their website.

http://www.italytravelandlife.com/

Photo Anthem Publishing- © iStock

For the most part, Italy has very little crime in the country. They tend to 'harden' their homes to prevent break-ins. All homes appear to have bars or automatic shutters that prevent break-ins. I asked a local, and he stated they never have break-ins. Well, no wonder. How would you? Violent crime, from what we have seen, is non-existent. They have very few muggings, robberies, break-ins, assaults, or murders. You see the local police, in their nicely pressed uniforms (very well built - wife's words), and they are very friendly. Of course, the police carry automatic assault weapons strung over their shoulders. Italian banks – now that's an adventure! You can't even get into the banks without unloading your cell phones and any metal before being allowed in. You enter a small windowed room that they scan; if it shows positive like a TSA scan, you can't come in. My observation is Italians attempt to prevent crime in the first place. If you can't break-in, you don't try, and you move on. They have a different concept on preventing crime. And it seems to make good sense.

Chapter 2
Traveling in Italy
Prego (Pray-go)
You're welcome

Tickets

When arriving in Italy, you can stop in a Tobacco (Tabacchi) shop to purchase bus tickets, phone cards, and other items you will need for your journey throughout Italy. There is no shortage of these shops in Italy and are quite easy to find.

Distance

327 miles – Rome to Venice

246 miles – Venice to Cinque Terre

284 miles – Rome to Cinque Terre

16 minutes – Monterosso al Mare to Riomaggiore by train/ 34 minutes by car with little or no parking/ 34 minutes by ferry

---

Trains

I love the trains in Italy; most are efficient, clean and modern. The major train stations, notably Rome and Milan, employ the latest technology with schedules displayed electronically on a large board plus television screens to assist the traveler. When using the system, be sure to review the timetable thoroughly with the track (binario) listed on where to board. Not paying close attention to the correct track number may result in an extended trip to central Italy versus north of Rome and a late-night check-in.

Forget about the stories of Italians being late. I have found their train system along with other transportation systems, to be quite punctual. If the train is scheduled to leave at 9:00, it leaves at 9:00. If you arrive exactly at 9:00, you will get to watch the train as it pulls away.

While most trains in Italy travel close to the same speed as in the U.S., there are a couple of exceptions. High-speed trains that travel between the major cities, such as Rome, Milan or Venice, can go up to speeds of 200 mph! These are quite modern and a joy to ride on.

In Italy, bars are mostly coffee houses, with snacks, and of course wine. Usually operating with only a couple of employees, you order, then pay when done; if you sit at a table, generally there is a surcharge. No one is in a rush, so you need to leave your American impatience behind.

You hear the conversations inside, sometimes with loud voices, but this is what Italians do. They will often have some insane soap box show on the television, but how can you criticize their shows compared to ours? Sitting in one of the chairs on the edge of the street, I watched people and cars go by, all within feet (or inches) of each other, with no one getting excited. While walking, if you hear tires behind you, you move. In some cases, quite quickly.

The smaller train stations are clean and efficient with television screens and printed schedules posted to assist the traveler; however, don't be put off too much about the graffiti that seems to be everywhere. Most may have a small bar where you can purchase an espresso, snacks, or a glass of vino. However, we have found several bathrooms that are less than desirable. Most public restrooms lack toilet seats and even  toilet paper (much to my wife's chagrin); some even lack a toilet and consists of a porcelain hole on the floor. It is always a good idea to carry an extra tissue with you when visiting these facilities. Restrooms in the larger cities, require a small amount of money to enter, usually one euro which is an excellent investment to ensure you have the essential necessities of a bathroom!

Wine Tasting

Here in the U.S., we are accustomed to visiting the various wineries in a region without making reservations; just show up and taste the varieties of wine at the winery. In Italy, one must make reservations at a local winery in advance. Often a local tour will advertise these type of wine tours, and they are an excellent way to go. We have had some fascinating and amusing adventures with other couples from America on such a wine tour. You will also find that in most instances, you and your small group will be the only ones at the winery. For more information on wine and tours, visit Chapter 3 of this book.

Picking the Grapes

Outside Orvieto, we ran across this machine that went up and down the rows and stripped the grapes from the vines. They were then dumped into a large container and transported for processing.

Subway – Rome

The subway system in Rome is extremely efficient, economical and easy to understand. You purchase the ticket at the station or a nearby Tobacco shop, insert the ticket for entry and board the subway train. If you plan on touring Rome, this is the best and most economical way to visit this gorgeous city. I do have one word of warning, and that is to be aware of pickpockets.

Always be alert of your surroundings and keep your belongings in a money belt. Follow the same rules for traveling around the city on foot.

Note the picture above; this is not the regular appearance of the Roman train. It's more of the exception, rather than the rule. But it did make for a great picture!

Eating in Italy
Do you like bacon, eggs, grits, and potatoes for breakfast? Well, don't look for these items in Italy. Typically, you will get thinly sliced meats, prosciutto, cereal, yogurt, boiled eggs, bread and maybe some fruit. I hate to say it, but when we get to a large city that has a Burger King or McDonald's, we quickly make our way there and order an Egg McMuffin. I did find one place that made 'American' omelets, but for some reason, it required a pound of salt by the cook; this may be their way of discouraging a repeat of the order.

For dinner, you may find that most restaurants open around 7 pm with diners arriving near 8 pm. I found, notably, in the smaller villages, that arriving promptly at 7 pm when they first open, is somewhat irritating to the restaurant workers as they are still preparing the food for the evening. Waiting until 7:30 appears to be more acceptable. One thing you need to understand about Italian food is that it is not fast food. Bring your patience but rest assured you will be well-rewarded. The food is fantastic, with the only issue of keeping your waistline in check while on vacation. That's where walking will pay off. Bring a good pair of walking shoes and enjoy the scenery.

> We go into a nice restaurant, and the wife needs to use the restroom. Located downstairs, she walks down the stairs and tries two doors that are locked, but finds one that isn't. She goes in, the door closes behind her, and she sees that she is in a broom closet. She turns around....and the door has locked behind her. She can't get out! She hears someone coming out of the bathroom next door, and she taps the door. *"Hello... hello... can you let me out?"* A young foreign girl cautiously opens the door so she can exit. In the meantime, I am upstairs, and I hear this knocking downstairs. *"I wonder what that is all about?"* I ask myself. Then I find out. It's all part of the great adventure. *(printed with permission from the wife of course)*

Another alternative to dinner is the local tapas. These small, bite-sized meals are served in many of the local bars hours before the 8:00 dinner rush. Often simply served with toothpicks, these tapas are usually quite tasty and in some places with quite a variety of different samples. With my less-than-perfect command of the Italian language, I simply point to what I desire and smile. I highly recommend this route as you can get a variety of small tastings for a nominal price. Of course, as with the meals, good wine is the paired drink. We fit in quite nicely.

A sign of the times...rooms for rent are in English, Italian, and German. But they may want to think about Chinese. There are many Chinese tourists here - an indication of their economic wealth that didn't exist a few years ago. Which reminds me... I go into the Hertz car rental in La Spezia, south of Cinque Terre, to turn in the car. I am waiting while a young Chinese woman in front of me is talking to a Hertz rep on the phone. She sees me and quickly asks *"do you speak English?"* to which I replied positively. She immediately asks if I can talk to the rep as she is having language problems. My problem is... the Hertz rep is Italian and I can't understand her poor English.

I try a little and then give the phone back. But the customer is frustrated. She got rear-ended and doesn't know how to explain it. With hand motions and drawings including pointing to cars out on the street, I understand what had occurred and advise her what to write on the Hertz accident form. She asks some additional questions, and I give my best advice. She is grateful, and she and her friend try to help me carry my luggage out to the taxi; which I do not need, but they are determined to do something to show their appreciation.

It is customary to not tip in Italy; sometimes it is included in the bill. Check the menu to see if the tip is included. Most often, if it isn't included in the bill, then 5-10% is acceptable.   Tipping excessively in restaurants or cafes is often frowned upon. Tipping is only a concern where waiters and waitresses work, if you order food at a counter, then no tip is expected. Also in those instances when you are at a coffee shop where most Italians stand, then sitting at a table will include a surcharge. Frankly, I would rather pay the extra charge in order to sit at a table enjoying my Americano.

Rental Car

Driving a rental car in Italy can be a frightening experience. Traffic rules seem not to apply, and the road signs can be confusing. Out in the country, highway speed limits and highway lane markers appear to be simply a suggestion to many of the drivers. Motorcycles are like mosquitos, driving everywhere including shoulders and between cars. As a visitor told me at the rental car agency in La Spezia, *"these Italians drive crazy!"*

I did find that not understanding Italian can be a blessing! A fast-moving motorcyclist in Rome came up upon us out of nowhere, and due to his high rate of speed and my turning into his lane, it was exciting, to say the least! I discovered you don't get all that upset when someone is screaming at you in a foreign language! I just smiled and waved as he angrily drove off, frustrated at my lack of reaction.

Do you need to drive in a large city such as Rome or Milan? I highly recommend against it. It is easy to get lost, street names change even if you haven't turned anywhere, and parking is non-existent. I have driven for hours in both cities, frustrated at the lack of parking spaces, let alone even a place to temporarily stop and look at a map. Most Italian cities have excellent mass transit that is punctual and economical to use.

Outside the cities, the train system is an efficient mode of transportation should you be going to one of the major tourist sites, such as Venice or Cinque Terre. The trains are comfortable, economical and punctual. I need to stress punctual; if you show up one minute late, the train 'has left the station.'

However, if you desire to travel to the smaller villages of Italy, notably Tuscany, then a rental car is the only way to go unless you go with a tour group. If traveling to just the major cities of Italy you may miss the essence, the quaintness, beauty, and the history of Italy. All the Italian regions have unique characteristics which can only be visited by car.

> Know how to tick off an Italian driver? Go 15 kilometers above the speed limit. It slows them down.

As I previously mentioned, when renting a car, I recommend traveling to a small village where entry to the Italian road system is easier to access. I can't count the number of times I left a major city only to drive around trying to find the highway or even where to return the rental car; Rome and Milan were the most difficult. When visiting in the Piedmont Region, I prefer to rent a car in Alba, a community of around 32,000 population, where the rental car agency is located about a quarter mile away from the train station and entry to the nearby highway system is easy.

The size of the rental car will depend on how much luggage you have and how many riders, but keep in mind that parking in any city can be challenging. Regarding insurance, my own insurance company here in the states recommended I purchase the auto insurance offered in Italy by the rental car agency. As far as which auto rental agency to use, I reserve with the major U.S. companies; online reviews of the various auto rental agencies can be somewhat 'enlightening' with complaints ranging from over-charging to being charged for damages even though rust existed on the damaged part. I want a company that is reputable and honest. Renting a car through AAA gave me an additional reliable resource for any potential auto issues that might have arisen.

You should review in advance where your rental car agency is located. I once selected the Turin Airport as I 'assumed' it was close to Turin (Torino). What I didn't research was the actual distance from Turin to the airport. The sixty-minute ride from the train station to the airport parking facility cost me over a hundred euro.

When returning a rental car I recommend you use your cell phone or camera, to take pictures of every side of the car including the underside. Should there be a question regarding damages, you have some evidence to support your claim. Horror stories abound of unreputable rental car agencies trying to charge people for damages they did not incur. Again, this is another example of why you should go through a reputable American auto rental company, or through AAA for your reservations.

Road Signs

Stop signs are where drivers come to a complete stop. You would think this is a no-brainer, right? Wrong. Just be aware that some drivers treat stop signs as a suggestion, rather than a requirement. The same can be said about posted speed limits.

You should also be aware of the different colored road signs. A green sign means that the road is an Autostrada (basically a freeway). Most, if not all, autostradas come with a toll at the exit. Taking the toll card you received upon entry onto the freeway, put it into the machine where the total amount due will appear on the screen. Then, insert your credit card, or coins, into the machine, and the gate will open. Blue signs are main highways that are a bit slower than autostradas but have no road tolls. Restaurant signs are either yellow or white while churches, places of interest, and tourist destinations are most often shown as brown. Everything else is white. It is highly recommended that if you plan on driving in Italy, you become thoroughly familiar with Italian signs. Not doing so could result in an accident, speeding ticket or having your car towed. Any of these instances would most definitely put a damper on your dream vacation.

Should you use GPS? I would say the answer is yes. I can't count the number of times I got lost trying to read the road signs while driving.

Adventures

If you do rent a car, you most undoubtedly will have different experiences than what one would experience on the train.

Driving in Rome and other major Italian cities can be challenging! Names of street signs appear to change on every block making it EASY to get lost. The speed limit is a mere suggestion as are stop signs and painted lines on the road. Add in dozens of pedestrians darting in and out of traffic to the mix, and you have the ingredients for an extremely stressful drive. My wife frequently closes her eyes while I am driving so she can enjoy the ride without the fear of injury!

Evening Passeggiata ("The little walk"). It takes the Italians to create a great event from a simple stroll. On most nights between the hours of 5 and 7 pm, Italians love to take a relaxing stroll on some of their main streets of Italy, walking, visiting, laughing and just simply enjoying life.

When in Rome you can find these walks along the famous shopping area of Via del Corso or in the trendy neighborhood of Trastevere. Whether in Rome, or other communities such as Orvieto, Pavia, or the eastern coastal city of San Benedetto Del Tronto, be sure to enjoy the passeggiata. For me, it was one of the most delightful experiences one can enjoy. People stroll, often arm in arm, window shopping, or just socializing with each other. Some dress up, some don't. Who cares? It's just people enjoying life.

Getting Lost

Despite several trips to Italy, I still get lost, when driving. Trying to figure out the road and map systems, puzzling arrows, lack of signs, crazy drivers going twice the speed limit. But, do not be intimidated. It's all worth the adventure. Keep your cool, backtrack as needed, and take your time. People are gracious and willing to help.

If riding the train and you fail to understand the schedule, you may end up going in the wrong direction. The key point here is that when you realize you are going in the wrong direction, get off at the next medium-sized train station. Some stations have only one train arrival per day, and it can be a long wait if you get off at a small station. While you wait for the next train, simply cozy up to the local bar and enjoy a glass of wine, much like we did when we traveled three hours east of Rome instead of north. Or if you are in Venice, where the bed and breakfast owner assured us we could not get lost, (only temporarily misguided) he stated: "You are on an island!" No reason to get excited, you are just 'misplaced.'

Taxis

When traveling in a large city such as Rome, Milan, Naples or Turin, you have several choices of transportation including buses, trains, and taxis. Trains are the easiest to navigate and are quite easy on the wallet.

However, if you need to get somewhere quickly, the local taxis may be your best solution. They aren't overly expensive provided you select a city-sponsored taxi. I would caution that if you have a fear of dying, you may want to just observe through your side window rather than looking directly forward, where all the action is. Most Italians drive notoriously fast, and that includes taxis. I am always amazed though, at the lack of car accidents.

> There is a scene in Chevy Chase's movie 'European Vacation' where he is driving in Italy and comes upon a group of racing bicyclists, forcing many off the road. While I won't admit to doing anything similar, there is a section of Italy I should probably not visit again.

A final note: when giving directions to the taxi driver, for any situation, be aware that not all drivers fully understand English. When leaving Turin for the airport, my driver had a hard time understanding the word 'Hertz' for the rental car agency. In Italian, the letter 'e' sounds like the letter 'a.' After several minutes of hand motions, he finally understood, and we proceeded to the agency 'Hartz.'

City Bus
In most circumstances, I don't take a bus for transportation as I prefer a taxi for a more direct and quick transport. But I have before and have found the bus to be comfortable, clean and punctual. Along with other transportation systems in Italy, tickets must be punched and validated before boarding, or you can face a hefty fine. There is nothing more entertaining than seeing a group of college students all lined up on a bus frantically trying to punch their tickets on the single machine with an enforcement officer slowly making his way onto the bus!

Teenagers. Ya gotta love them. My first visit to Italy included our two teenagers and their friend. I can verify that taking a vacation with three fifteen-year-olds has it "challenges." Whether it was the giggling, poking each other, or them watching the nonstop, mindless Italian music television programs, it was enough to test anyone's patience. So off we go on more sight-seeing, rather than staying back at the apartment, despite the fact I can hardly walk trying to keep up with them the previous day! The pain was more endurable than the giggling.

Water Taxis

When visiting water-related tourism sites, you will find that water taxis are usually the most economical and expedient way for traveling to the destination. We found those in the Cinque Terre region to be extremely punctual; as noted with train schedules, if the boat is slated to leave at 9:00 am, it leaves at 9:00 am. I have seen cases of tourists running up the dock and the boat operators didn't even slow down as we departed the shore. Once you arrive at your destination, be sure to exit immediately. They get excited if you are slow to exit, as we found out in Cinque Terre. On a positive note regarding water taxis, if you miss one boat, have patience; there is another scheduled to arrive shortly. The transport itself is a scenic ride, and the boats are clean, with decent seats.

With the canal system in Venice, they city employs water 'buses.' Commonly called Vaporettos, these boats are used to transport the thousands of visitors daily, throughout the city. As with other Italian modes of transportation, these are efficient and punctual; later in the day, you will find them crowded. To buy a ticket, purchase it at one of their nearby booths, validate it at a nearby machine at the time of use, then get on the boat when it arrives. You may purchase one-way tickets, or a ticket for a longer period (i.e. 24, 48 hours). I recommend buying a ticket for the length of your stay; you will find that Venice is a large city with confusing streets. Utilizing the Vaporetto will save you countless hours of mindless walking, trying to locate whatever destination you are trying to reach. A 24-hour ticket price will range around 20 euro in cost. Again, remember to punch your ticket before getting on the boat. If you are checked by an enforcement officer, and you have not, you will get a costly violation notice for failing to validate. To avoid a fine, merely put the ticket in a nearby machine, and it will stamp the time and date.

Restrooms

While it may seem somewhat ridiculous to mention restroom use in Italy, it is an important bit of information to know as a first-time visitor. My first trip to Italy I encountered a public restroom that I had to pay to enter. Of course, I was incensed, why should I pay? Well, you quickly learn that it is a pleasure to pay to ensure you have a seat and toilet paper. Note that some public restrooms are simply a hole in the ground. As my wife said the first time she was expected to utilize such a restroom, "Not in this life!" Although, when you get right down to it, it all depends on the urgency of the situation!

We became accustomed to taking care of 'business' before we left the lodging for the day. As most restaurants have decent restrooms for customers only, we would stop by for a quick bite or a glass of wine, and utilize their facilities. When asked why toilet tissue was so scarce, a lodge owner in Montepulciano shrugged his shoulder and stated that the gypsies steal the seats and toilet paper; whether this is true, I cannot say. As mentioned earlier, it may seem crazy that I even need to discuss it, but this could be a crucially important subject.

Street Musicians and Entertainers

Whether in Rome, Venice or any other city in Italy, you will find an assortment of street musicians and entertainers.

Many are quite good and remarkable in their talents and deserve a tip for their skills and entertainment.

Some, like the costumed Gladiators, I merely avoided. Stopping by to take a picture involved the expectation of a generous tip.

Chapter 3
Vino and Tours

Come stai?   (Comay Sty?)
How are you?

Wine, wine, wine. Few countries have such a variety of great wines as the country of Italy. While you could write a complete book just on Italian wines, below are a few of our favorites when traveling through Italy.

> With my first visit to Italy, my 15-year-old teenager insisted that when she arrived in Italy, she was going to have a glass of wine because it was legal. I agreed, and at our first meal in Rome, she began to order some wine. I stopped her and told her to take a sip of mine first. She did, and her response was "Yuck." That took care of that issue.

Notable Wines

Barbera.   Grown in the Piedmont region of Italy, this wine is acknowledged as the third-most grown grape variety in Italy. With hints of dark cherry, dried strawberry, plum, and blackberry to name a few, this wine is often referred to as the "wine of the people." Aged 2-4 years, the wine is reasonably economical to purchase making it quite popular. The wine also goes by Italian geographical names such as Barbera d'Alba, Barbera d'Aosta, Barbera Sarda, Barbera d'Asti, and Barbera del Monferrato. While staying at a B&B in central Piedmont one year, we were given our first bottle of Barbera where we fell in love with this most pleasing wine. For some reason, it didn't last long.

Barolo.   Known as the "King of Wines" for centuries and produced from the native Nebbiolo grape, then aged for 2-3 years. Grown in the hills surrounding the village of Barolo in the Piedmont Region, the wine has hints of cherry, truffles, and roses with a rather light color and requires several years of aging in barrel and bottle. By law, Barolo must age a minimum of three years or at least two in a barrel. The village itself sits in a beautiful setting on a hill overlooking the vineyards surrounding the entire town. If ever in Barolo, you must stop in and visit their high-tech museum on wine.

Barbaresco. Historically named the Nebbiolo di Barbaresco after the grape it is made from, Barbaresco grows near the city of Alba and its namesake Barbaresco, located in the Piedmont region. Somewhat similar in texture to the Barolo wine, Barbaresco comes from a warmer, drier and milder climate with a slight maritime climate. With these conditions, the grapes tend to ripen earlier than Barolo and results in wines that are less tannic and more drinkable at an earlier age. If ever visiting this region, time it so you can attend the unforgettable and impressive Truffle Festival in Alba, an annual month-long international event held in October each year.

Dolcetto. Grown alongside the Barbera and Nebbiolo grapes in the Piedmont region, the name means "little sweet one," referring not to the sweetness of the wine, but to the ease of growing and making good wines. This wine possesses flavors of concord grape, wild blackberries, and herbs.

Vino Nobile di Montepulciano. Aged for two years and made from the Sangiovese grape varietal and blended with Canaiolo Nero and small amounts of other varieties such as Mammolo. The grapes grow in the Tuscany area near Montepulciano, a beautiful village sitting on top of a hill overlooking the gorgeous valley surrounding the town.

Brunello di Montalcino. Produced in the vineyards surrounding the beautiful Tuscan town of Montalcino, this red wine is quite popular and can be one of the more expensive wines to purchase. Montalcino has a warmer and drier climate than its neighbor Montepulciano resulting in the grapes ripening a week earlier. Brunello di Montalcino is made from 100% Sangiovese and is aged for three years. For a perfect lunch, stop by one of the quaint restaurants in the village, eat a fantastic meal and enjoy a glass of Brunello di Montalcino while looking out over the scenic valley.

Garganega. Known as one of Italy's more admired wines, Garganega is a white varietal grown near Veneto in northern Italy. It forms the basis of the Venetian white wine Soave.

Chianti. Chianti is any wine produced in the Chianti region located in Tuscany. You have probably seen the original packaging of Chianti in the squat bottle enclosed in a straw basket, called a fiasco or 'flask' in English. These days Chianti is bottled in the more standard shaped wine bottles. Made of at least 80% Sangiovese, Chianti is aged for at least 38 months.

Sciacchetrà. A dessert wine from the Cinque Terre area, this wine is kept in cellars, saved for special occasions such as weddings and baptisms. As is the case of most grapes grown in Cinque Terre, this is a white wine. Sciacchetrà is well worth the taste if you can find it at a local restaurant.

Prosecco. Italy's most prevalent sparkling wine, Prosecco is often compared to Champagne but is made from a different set of grapes and a different winemaking method. Mostly grown near the town of Veneto, this wine is made from Prosecco grapes and is often produced in a dry, *brut* style. However, coupled with flavors of green apple, honeydew melon, pear, and honeysuckle, this wine tastes sweeter than what one would expect. Often a favorite for a morning mimosa, it is best served two parts sparkling wine to 1-part juice.

Limoncello. One of Italy's more well-liked liqueur, this drink is often served chilled after dinner as a *digestive (after dinner drink)*. Limoncello is made from lemon peels; the juice is mixed with simple syrup along with sugar and water. Not bitter as found with lemons, nothing warms you faster than a small glass of limoncello on a cold, Italian night. Alcohol content can be as much as 26%, notably with home-made variants.

Grappa. When I am asked to describe grappa, I would often ask if the person has tried 'white lightning.' With an alcohol content of 35 to 60%, this drink will most definitely curl your toes. Forty million bottles of grappa are produced in Italy each year of this well-liked drink. This drink is made from discarded grape seeds, stalks and stems left over from the winemaking process; and has been around for centuries. For a real morning pick-me-up, try the "café corretto." Both Grappa and Prosecco are popular drinks in Venice.

The first time I tasted grappa was with the Italian owner of a Bed and Breakfast in Tuscany. Between the wine and the grappa, his English turned quite comical and my attempt at Italian was equally as bad, if not worse. Another memorable experience in Italy!

Bellini. Not a type of wine, but more of a cocktail consumed mostly in Venice. Made of white wine and peach juice, Bellini is made with champagne and peach juice with a touch of raspberry to add the pink color; sometimes prosecco is used instead of champagne.

Valpolicella. This wine is a rather light, easy-to-drink red with hints of blueberries and banana. Grown in the Veneto region near Venice, this wine is quite popular with pasta. The wine is enjoyed at room temperature or slightly chilled.

Remember, unlike in America where you can show up unannounced, Italian wineries customarily require a reservation; and that is if they offer tastings. The recommended way to taste these great wines are through tours that are offered throughout the region.

Tours

To fully understand Rome and its history, one must sign up for any of the dozens of tours offered throughout Italy. We had visited Rome before and walked about without an organized sightseeing visit, but you fail to comprehend the extensive history of this great, ancient city. The tours we utilized have been well organized with outstanding guides. Before signing for one of these outings, check the reviews for each company on the web and select the one tour that best suits what your desires are. One tour guide mentioned to me that before the Internet, there were some shady operators in the business. Due to online reviews, many of those operators were forced out of the trade.

Below are some recommendations, a small sampling of the dozens of tours offered in Italy.

Rome and the Surrounding Area

Through Eternity Tours.
(www.througheternity.com) This company offers dozens of tours of not only Rome but other cities as well.

Viator (www.viator.com)
A TripAdvisor company, Viator offers an assortment of tours including many wine tours. These tours will often include transportation and food.

Dark Rome (www.darkrome.com or www.citywonders.com)
With several thousand reviews of 5 stars, this company also conducts many various, entertaining tours. We had utilized Dark Rome before and loved each one.

Rick Steves (www.ricksteves.com)
Internationally known and author of dozens of travel books, Rick Steves also offers tours to Italy and other European vacation spots. Outstanding story teller, Rick Steves shows are frequently seen on PBS.

Citalia (www.citalia.com) With over 85 years of experience, Citalia comes highly recommended from various sources.

Perillo Tours (www.perillotours.com) Decades of traveling in Italy, Perillo comes highly recommended for specialized and customized tours.

Below are some examples of possible tours that may be offered:

Rome and Colosseum Walking Tour. If visiting the Colosseum, then a guide is a must to understand and appreciate the history of this magnificent structure fully. Located next door to the Colosseum, one needs to visit the Roman Forum, often called the Roman ruins. Both locations offer a photographer's dream of capturing ancient Rome with beautiful pictures.

Pompei and Mount Vesuvius. Close to an all-day tour, Pompei is fascinating to walk about observing how life must have been before the disastrous eruption of Mount Vesuvius, destroying the city in its wake.

Vatican and St. Peters Basilica. Years ago, you could just breeze in, pay the small admission fee, and visit for hours. Today you need to go through long security lines to gain entrance. I highly recommend you sign up for a tour versus waiting in line for an hour or so.

Borghese Gallery. The paintings are magnificent and overwhelming. You need a tour guide.

Food and Wine Tours. Most, if not all, of the tour companies, will offer an assortment of food and wine tours. We love these tours and highly recommend them. Some will require walking; others may involve transportation to a site outside Rome. As appears to be the norm, the food and wine served are always outstanding.

Tuscany. Some companies will offer day trips to the beautiful Tuscany region; an excellent way to visit this area if you do not have a car. Many areas of Tuscany are not accessible by train, so either you drive or sign up for a tour. As I have driven in Tuscany before, I would vote for the tour.

There are some excursions to villages of Montepulciano, Bagno Vignoni and Montalcino, the latter famous for its Brunello wine while Montepulciano is well known for its Vino di Nobile wine. Even outside any wine tastings, these three villages are some of the most beautiful to visit. In Bagno Vignoni put your feet into one of the rock ditches and soak. Your feet will thank you. What a treat! In Montalcino, relax, sit back, and enjoy eating and drinking in a beautiful setting.

I was at a nearby Vatican restaurant, of which there are many, I had asked for the check, "mi scusi, il conto per favore", which means "the check, please." Except I was pronouncing it "il canto" which, as the waitress laughed, means "Do you want to sing?" she exclaimed, waving her arms in the way only Italians can do. Canto, Conto. Whatever. It is all about living the Italian dream. Laugh, save the memory and move on.

Cinque Terre
Cinque Terre has a variety of tours available; most involve walking, food, and wine.

Enoteca Internazionale

The oldest wine store in Monterosso, the Enoteca Internazionale offers an assortment of local, Italian and international wines along with olive oils and other products of Cinque Terre. Wine tastings are provided by professionals for either individuals or groups; reservations are requested. Many of the local wines are presented including the dessert wine Sciacchetra. This enoteca offers indoor and outdoor seating where you can try other delicious food items such as the bruschetta (must try the ones with the local anchovies), chutneys, great salads and even desserts.

> Address: 19016 Monterosso al Mare
> http://www.enotecainternazionale.com/e
> noteca-en.html

Angelos Boat Tours

Highly rated boat tour of the Cinque Terre coastline, this trip is a must-see for those wanting to capture the best photography of the five villages. To top it off, the operators offer a great lunch to boot or an evening tour with tapas and prosecco (Italian champagne). Private tours, with up to 10 people, can also be arranged. Located in Monterosso Harbor.

Owners Alessandro Cinque and wife Brenda can be contacted at info@angelosboattours.com

http://www.angelosboattours.com/home

(+39) 333-687-9249

Voyager Tours

Another highly rated tour in the Cinque Terre, Voyager offers a variety of tours personalized to your tastes. Prices and tour information: voyagertrips@gmail.com

http://voyagertrips.com/personalized-day-tours/

(+39) 346-755-3978

Venice

There are lots of tours offered in Venice, many of the previously mentioned tour companies offer a variety of tours in Venice and the surrounding area. Check out their websites for a listing.

Tours by Locals.com

Along with those companies previously mentioned, we highly recommend Elisabetta Amadi of *"Tours by local.com."* Excellent and friendly host in Venice, very knowledgeable of the local area, you walk away like you have known her all your life.

guide_9517-110@toursbylocals.com

(+39) 349-874-5250

"ViniItaly"

Held in nearby Verona, this festival is held the second weekend of April. "ViniItaly" is the most premier and largest wine exhibition in the world. Over 4000 exhibitors from over 27 countries attend this event, showcasing their excellent wines. Daily wine tasting takes place with lessons for those wanting to learn (aren't we all?). Tickets for 2017 were around 120 euro for this four-day event, free for disabled and anyone accompanying them. For more information, see their website at http://www.vinitaly.com/en

Other
"Cantine Aperte"

While in the U.S. most wineries have tasting rooms with regular open schedules. That is not the case in Italy, where reservations are often required to taste the local wines. However, once a year, over 800 wineries open their doors for "Cantine Aperte," Italian for "open cellars," an event that attracts over a million tourists a year. For more information on this event, along with many others, go to the *movimento turisomo vino* website at:
http://www.movimentoturismovino.it/en/home

Marco's Way Day Tours. Le Marche Region, south of Venice. This excellent and friendly guide does not rush the trip. Extensive knowledge of the region and the best places to visit including wineries and olive oil producers. One of our personal favorites.

http://www.marcosway.it/links.php
(+39) 32-8764-4253 or
email: info@marcosway.it

Touring in Italy. Okay, maybe they like us. But I found that when you sign up with a guide in some sections of Italy, don't count on the tour adhering to the selected advertised hours for the tour; it could easily be more hours for the same price! Italian tour guides do not appear to be in a hurry if they observe that you are enjoying yourself. They just sit back and experience the time with you. Tipping is always accepted, which seems to always occur after a couple of glasses of wine.

Chapter 4
Rome, the Vatican, Pompei, and Orvieto

Buongiorno (bwon jorno)
'Good morning' or 'Good day' as appropriate

The Vatican

Reason to visit

The Pope is here. The (church) is awe-inspiring, along with the museum. Visit the Vatican museums, Sistine Chapel, and St. Peter's Basilica. Take a tour and learn about the Renaissance artwork of masters including Michelangelo.

Location

Vatican City is located in a walled city within Rome, just east of the Trastevere area of Rome, which is another marvelous locale to roam. Situated on 110 acres with a population of just over 800, Vatican City is the smallest city, population and geographical wise, in the world.

Odds and Ends

It used to be easy to access the Vatican with short wait times to enter the building. That changed in 2016 with increased security needs. Due to the long lines to enter, this past year we passed up on visiting the Vatican. Much like the Coliseum, where reservations can expedite the entrance process, it is now recommended to do the same with the Vatican and other buildings. Tours can be signed up in advance, through trusted web internet sites such as TripAdvisor or tour guide expert Rick Steves.

Restaurants
La Pancia Felice. Close to the Vatican with excellent food. Small dining area but with friendly staff.

Address: Via di Porta Castello 11/12
Phone: (+39) 06 686 1819

Rome

How to get there
All roads lead to Rome. And Trains. And Planes.

Founded around the year 625 BC, Rome has a rich and colorful history second to none. With a current population of over 4.4 million residents, Rome remains one of the most visited cities in the world.

Sites to see

The Colosseum, the Roman Forum, the Vatican and museums, the Pantheon (and our personal favorite), Trevi Fountain, the Spanish Steps, the Sistine Chapel, Piazza Navona, St. Peter's Basilica, and the Galleria Borghese to name just a few of the great sites.

The best thing about Rome

It's extensive history, beautiful churches, fascinating ancient buildings, and great food and wine. Not to mention the warm and friendly people who reside in this great city.

Isernia, Italy. A city of over 20,000 residents, Isernia is located in the central region of Molise. It is about a 2-hour train ride east from Rome.

This city is also where you wind up in if you don't pay attention to the correct rail number for departure to Orvieto. One important lesson to remember is that if you do get on the wrong train, do not get off at the next station. It may be a stop that trains only frequent once a day due to the size of the town, which can also give you a clue on the chances of finding a hotel room. When you discover you are on the wrong train (Wife: *"What? Not again!"*), just remain on board until you see a good size city; then exit and check the train schedules going in the opposite direction. Most often a train will be going through in 2-4 hours; just sit down at the next-door bar, sip the wine, and enjoy the day. If trains are not going through until the next day, at least you should be able to find a nearby hotel room. Just go with the flow.

Traveling in Rome

For good exercise (notably after eating all that rich food), most of the tourist sights are within walking distance. The streets are safe, just be more alert in crowded situations due to some pickpockets who roam the crowds of tourists. Taxis are another service and reasonably priced as well, just be sure to take your heart medicine in advance (or drink a good glass of wine) to calm your nerves. Busses and trains are another transportation option; they are economical and efficient. Signs in the train stations are posted in both Italian and English.

The Food

The food here is fantastic with prices varying depending on the location. For good food and great deals, simply get off the beaten path to find the same quality of food and service. For a restaurant price shock, simply eat near one of the famous tourist sites that are frequented by thousands of tourists a day. I use TripAdvisor reviews to find top-rated restaurants at reasonable prices.

Restaurant Recommendations

Vaca Loca Restaurant. Located near the Hotel Castle (see lodging below), we have eaten here several times and have never left unsatisfied. They provide outstanding food and service in a comfortable setting. Restaurant specialties include steaks and pizza.

> **Address:** Via di Settebagni 722 - 00138 Rome
> Phone (+39) 06-888-7542

Pane Vino e San Daniele. Great food and service with good pasta dishes and excellent wine.

> **Address:** Piazza Mattei 16 | D, 00186
> Phone: (+39) 06-687-7147

Da Vito e Dina Restaurant. Very highly rated restaurant specializing in pizza, Italian, seafood, and Mediterranean foods. Located a few blocks from the Vatican.

> **Address:** Via Degli Scipioni 50 |
> Prati, 00192
> Phone: (+39) 06-3972-3293

Odds and Ends

Rome is a very safe to walk in with very little violent crime. When walking around crowds though, particularly around train stations, be aware of shady characters, who may or may not be looking to pick your pocket or purse. A money belt is a must when walking in crowded areas. A word of caution when crossing the street: look both ways, then look again. Mopeds and cars zigzag in all directions to present a significant challenge for crossing safely.

There are notable differences between the thousands of restaurants in Rome; many are outstanding, many are not. The same can be said for the cost of eating and drinking in Italy. Do your research, and you may avoid paying an exorbitant price for a croissant and a cup of Americano coffee.

A recent trend in Rome is 'combatting' food and drink at local tourist sites such as the Spanish Steps and ancient water fountains like the Piazza Navona; roughly 15 fountains in all. To ignore such rules  may bring a monetary fine by the local police. Swimming is forbidden in such fountains (notably the Trevi Fountain). Ignore what you viewed in the movie 'Roman Holiday,' if one attempts to break the rules, you will pay a fine.

Every summer between the months of June and September the shores of the Tiber River become a festival with tents of music, food, shopping, and even foosball. Every year millions of visitors visit this area near Trastevere neighborhood. A free event, it is quite enjoyable to sit at one of the many bars or restaurants and listen to the local music.

Nearby on Isola Tiberina (Tiber Island), an annual cinema festival takes place where foreign and Italian films are shown in the open air.

Pantheon

Constructed as a temple, and now a church, this 2000-year-old landmark is one of the most architecturally beautiful buildings you will ever see. Despite the age, the inside paintings still look fresh and quite impressive to view. The building appears rectangular from the outside, the inside is circular.

Looking up you will view the oculus, an engineering marvel in the Roman world. Huge in diameter, it is still lined with the original Roman bronze and is the primary source of light for the whole building. The oculus is never covered, with the rain falling into the interior and running off the slightly convex floor to the still functioning Roman drain pipes below.

Trevi Fountain

What is so special about Foosball tables? Known also as Table Football, foosball was invented in 1921 and initially became popular in the United States during the 1960s until the popularity died in the 1980s, most likely due to the introduction of the electronic video game. Strangely enough, the popularity didn't appear to wane in Italy; we found them everywhere: along the Tiber River in Rome or some of the more remote areas such as Bagno Vignoni. Obviously, it remains quite popular with the locals.

Located in the Trevi district of Rome, the fountain is in the center of the city. The fountain stands 86 feet high, 161 feet wide and is the largest Baroque fountain in Rome, not to mention one of the most famous in the world. The fountain has appeared in numerous films include the famous La Dolce Vita by director Federico Fellini.

Trivia note

Some movie buffs have wondered whether the fountain scene from the 2003 film 'Under the Tuscan Sun' was the Trevi Fountain. It is not, nor does such an actual fountain exist in Cortona as represented in the movie. It was merely a prop that was dismantled after the film was completed. The first time we visited Rome, the Trevi fountain was closed due to major restoration, which was finished in 2015; we did manage to visit it in 2016 along with hundreds of other tourists. If you want to see the local police get excited, just try dipping your feet into the fountain. The ear-splitting whistle still resonates in my memory. And no, it wasn't me.

Trastevere

Located across the Tiber River, lies the neighborhood of Trastevere. It is a medieval community with numerous business and restaurants; Trastevere transforms into an exciting community at night with tourists and locals, alike, visiting the local establishments or relaxing to people watch as they stroll about the streets. This area is our favorite for lodging whenever we stay in Rome.

While strolling about at night in the summer time, take a short walk to the nearby Tiber River where rows of tents line the river, selling goods, food, and entertaining with live music. Sit back, enjoy the wine, and listen to the music!

Spanish Steps

Completed in 1725, the 135 steps were first introduced to the American public in the 1953 movie "Roman Holiday" with Gregory Peck and Audrey Hepburn and has been featured in many movies along with numerous mentions in recording songs. At the time of the construction, it linked the Bourbon Spanish Embassy with a nearby church. Located near the center of Rome, it is surrounded by numerous shops and tourist sites.

At the base of the Spanish Steps lies the most famous shopping district in Rome, the Piazza di Spagna. Here you will find thousands of shoppers lining the streets gazing at the windows of designer lines such as Prada, Gucci,

Miu Miu, Versace and many, many others. The Via del Corso is particularly popular with tourists walking shoulder-to-shoulder on the sidewalk, gazing at the clothing, jewelry, and other expensive items with exorbitant prices.

Il Vittoriano

Known as the Monumento Nazionale a Vittorio Emanuele II, or more often as il Vittoriano, this building is a monument built to honor the first king of a unified Italy, Victor Emmanuel who received the crown in March of 1861. Easily observed while walking or driving around central Rome, the building is also referred to unflatteringly as "the wedding cake' or "the typewriter."

Roman Forum (Roman ruins).

Brief History

One of my favorite places to visit in Rome, this site is often referred to as the Forum and is host to over 4 and a half million visitors each year. This area was, for centuries, the heart of Roman public life where victories of war were celebrated and was considered the center of commercial life. Many of the most historic structures in Rome are here. Located in central Rome, this site is an easy walk, bus or subway ride depending on where you are staying.

Colosseum/Coliseum

History
The largest amphitheater ever built, this structure was constructed and completed in 82 A.D. Holding between 50,000 and 80, 000 spectators, the Colosseum hosted up to 65,000 spectators. It was used for gladiator battles along with public spectacles such as mock sea battles, executions, re-enactments of famous battles and other exhibits. One of the most popular tourist sites in Rome, the Colosseum is host to thousands of visitors each year.

Tips on getting in
You have two choices for entry; you can either stand in line for hours or register with a tour group to expedite your entry. The official website to sign up for tours is

www.coopculture.it/en ticket.cfm. We chose a tour advertised in one of Rick Steve's travel books, guided by a group of young Americans who gave a very informative tour of the Colosseum. Meeting on the side of the Colosseum early in the morning, we were quickly whisked inside for a good two-hour tour.

Villa Borghese Gardens

This exhibit is a must-see while in Rome. The gardens were planted in 1605 and given to the city of Rome in 1903. It is the third largest park in Rome comprised of 197 acres. The garden also contains several buildings and museums, notably the unforgettable Galleria Borghese and the Villa Medici.

Scala Sancta

Located adjacent to the Basilica of St. Lateran in Rome, the Scala Sancta, otherwise known as the 'Holy Stairway,' is believed to be the actual steps that Jesus climbed on the day he died. Thought to have been brought to Rome by Saint Helena, mother of Emperor Constantine in 334 A.D., thousands of Catholic followers come to this holy site each year, climbing the steps one knee at a time up the 28-step staircase. First mentioned in papal documents in year 844; Pope Pius IX restored the staircase in the mid-1800s.

Part of the great adventure is meeting others from outside the United States. Most appear pleasant and not overly concerned regarding our politics. As we have driven around the beautiful cities in this country, we have come across several U.S. flags displayed at tourist's sites. Tee-shirts and purses also bearing the U.S. flag, appear to be popular. Cafes and restaurants intermix their music with Americans songs, especially the older ones dating from the 70's and 80's. We met a lovely couple while dining near Orvieto- he was German, she was French, and they live in Switzerland (Hmmm.... neutral country so they don't fight?). He spoke excellent English as we visited about 20 minutes. Briefly, we discussed Civita di Bagnoregio, Italy, where the allies bombed the bridge in WWII..."Yes", he said with his thick German accent and a smile. "Typical, Germans built it, Americans destroyed it". Well okay...it was all done in good humor. But he liked us... he really liked us! (remember Sally Fields).

Interesting Facts about Rome

❖ SPQR stands for "Senatus Populusque Romanus" which means "The senate and the people of Rome." You will see this on many statues and buildings throughout Rome

❖ Rome is known throughout the world as the "Eternal city"

❖ Rome is the largest city in Italy with a population of around 3 million. At one time, it was the largest city in Europe until London surpassed it

❖ The founders of Rome, Romulus, and Remus, were twin brothers. Romulus killed his brother Remus

❖ Rome was named after Romulus in 753 BC, who became Rome's first ruler

❖ Some police in the province of Lazio, where Rome is located, drive Lamborghinis

❖ About 3000 euros are collected each night at the infamous Trevi Fountain; these coins are then donated to a Catholic charity to feed needy families

❖ Italy became a unified country in 1870 and Rome the capital

❖ Rome attracts over 12 million visitors a year

❖ The 12-month calendar was introduced by Julius Caesar in 46 BC

Pompei

Reason to visit

Nationally known throughout the world, Pompei was buried under 13 to 20 feet of volcanic ash and pumice from the eruption of Mount Vesuvius in 79 AD. The site went undiscovered for 1500 years until initially discovered in 1599 and later rediscovered 150 years after that. Objects that lay underneath the ash were preserved for centuries because of the lack of air and moisture. During the excavation of the city, plaster was used to fill voids in the ash layers that once held human bodies, revealing the exact position of the person when he or she died. It is a fascinating place to visit, where many of the rooms excavated

expose how life was lived during these early times. An estimated 2.5 million visitors arrive each year to visit the site. Excavations at the site continue to this day.

On one trip, we ate in the small village of Roccatederight (can you understand why I couldn't spell it without looking?). This community is near the villages of Sassofortino and Montemassi, with nearby villages of Massa Marittima, Giuncarico, Montepescali, and Sticciano. Remember these names – you'll be tested tomorrow.

How to get there

Located approximately 130 miles south of Rome near Naples, Pompei can be reached by car, or (I highly recommend), a tourist bus. Taking a tour will include the history of the various parts of the city. It's something you won't get on your own.

Mt Vesuvius

An active volcano located south of Rome and a little over 5 miles from Naples, Mt Vesuvius is infamous for its destruction of  Pompei in 79 AD. Many tours to Pompei also include a trip up the mountain as well.

Orvieto
Reason to visit

Beautiful hill village and church, great restaurants, easy to walk around. No rental car is required as Orvieto is a short train ride from Rome.

The best thing about Orvieto

We enjoy walking around the old town center, exploring the side streets and the many stores that encompass the city. During the daytime, you can join the crowds of tourists who come to Orvieto to shop and eat. In the early evening, the crowds have thinned out, and the walks are more enjoyable. I particularly like walking in the early morning hours, when you often have the streets to yourself as the shops begin to open.

How to get there

Arriving by train from Rome, you can easily get to the center of Orvieto with the local Funicolare, a cable car in front of the Orvieto railway station. After hours, the only way to get to the town center is by taxi; you don't want to walk the distance which is straight up the hill. The Funicolare passes through a rock tunnel and arrives at the historic town center in about 3 minutes. It runs every 10 minutes during the daytime to 8:30 pm; during weekends, it runs every 15 minutes.

Sites to see
The Duomo

The main attraction in Orvieto is the Cathedral of Saint Mary of the Assumption (more commonly known as the Duomo. It is undoubtedly the town's most significant and unrivaled wonder. This Cathedral represents one of the great masterpieces of the  Italian Middle Ages. Built over the course of several centuries, from the thirteenth to the seventeenth, the Duomo is an impressive architectural marvel and a must-see when in Orvieto.

St. Patricks Well in Orvieto was built at the request of Pope Clement VII around the year 1520 to ensure the city would have water in case it was attacked. An engineering marvel, the well has 247 steps down with another stairway of 247 steps up; all one-way so you don't need to go around others walking in the opposite direction. Try to picture women with donkeys going down to the well, retrieving water and then going back up. The well took ten years to build.

Restaurants
Il Malandrino Bistrot. This restaurant offers outdoor and indoor sitting, we ate one of our best meals in Italy here. The staff was pleasant and outgoing, and service and food were excellent! Menu items include pasta, steak,

pizza, and wine often accompanied with live music. What else could you want?

Address: Via Garibaldi 20, 05018
Phone: (+39) 0763-344315

Trattoria La Grotta.   Lovely restaurant located on one of the side streets of the town; it is located close to the center of the village. Excellent Italian food with great service.

Address: Via Luca Signorelli 5, 05018
Phone: (+39) 0763-341348

Chapter 5
The Cinque Terre

Quanto costa? (Quan toe ko sta)
How much does it cost?

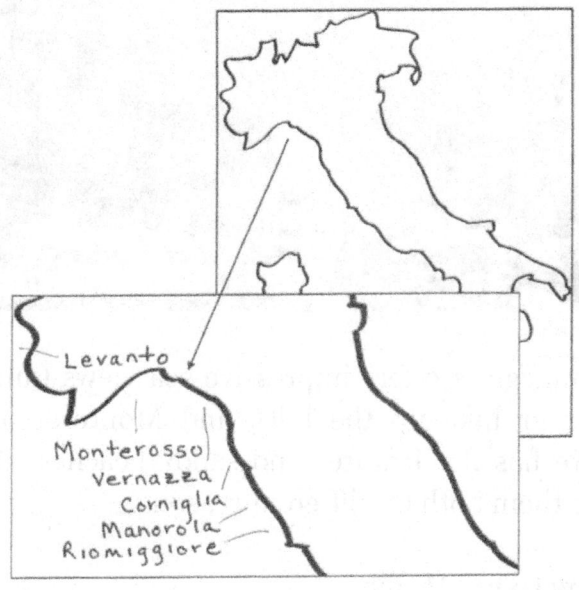

The Cinque Terre is comprised of five villages: Monterosso al Mare, Vernazza, Corniglia, Manarola, and Riomaggiore. The coastline, the five villages, and the surrounding hillsides are all part of the Cinque Terre National Park.

Each of the five villages offers distinct differences to visitors wanting to stay in the area. We have stayed at two of the villages and loved them both: Riomaggiore and Monterosso al Mare.

Riomaggiore offers impressive sea views (and a tougher hike up the hill), and Monterosso al Mare has flat features and sandy beaches. We love them both for different reasons.

How to get there
The train is the only sensible way to visit the Cinque Terre. Car travel in any of the towns is severely restricted with very limited parking available. There are some areas of Monterosso to drive and park, but forget about the rest. Our host in Riomaggiore has a car but is restricted to what roads she can drive on. Train travel between any of the villages only takes 2-5 minutes at the most. Train travel between Milan and Monterosso takes 3-4 hours and can cost

around $30-45. Booking a couple of months in advance can save you around 60%.

> Something to remember about Italy. The trains run exactly on time. So... if a train shows up 15 minutes early...it's the wrong train!!! I'm not saying I did it, but at least it was on the same line, and we didn't backtrack. As the wife said..."*What? Not again!*" (She says that a lot for good reason)

What to see

Most people who visit the Cinque Terre come to hike the infamous trail of the Cinque Terre National Park, which is a coastal hike between the five towns with breathtaking views of the coast and water. Initially the trails were set up as transportation routes between agricultural lands, villages, and sanctuaries. A nominal cost is required to hike the trail. At the time of this writing, the trail between Manarola and Riomaggiore (Via dell' Amore) was still closed due to winter landslide damages from several years ago. The last update is that work is to commence this fall (2017) with completion the early part of 2019.

While hiking, ensure you have adequate shoes and be prepared for some sections that can be somewhat challenging.

Other reasons to visit: the beauty of the area. The sunsets are amazing, and each village is a picture postcard to send home. You could easily spend a month here exploring each of the communities, and getting your exercise after eating the great food!

Where to stay
All have distinct advantages. We prefer Riomaggiore for the fantastic view of the town and of the sea; Monterosso we love because of the beach and the fact most of the town is somewhat flat making for easier walking. For the younger crowd, Monterosso and Vernazza are the primary choices for the more active nightlife. See Tab B at the end of this book for my lodging recommendations. For additional hotels, bed and breakfasts, or apartment choices, check out TripAdvisor or Booking.com for reviews not to mention Homeaway.com or Airbnb.

Riomaggiore

Dating from the thirteenth century, Riomaggiore is known for its wine and historic character. Sitting on the edge of the Sea of Genoa, one can gaze at some of the bluest waters you will ever see. Having a glass of wine doesn't hurt either.

How to get there

If you are short on brain cells, you may attempt to drive here. Don't. Parking is non-existent, and the roads cannot accommodate many cars. The few streets in town require an approved authorization, failure to have the correct pass will result in a hefty fine. Rail is the primary mode and is an excellent way to arrive at one of the most interesting and beautiful Italian towns you will discover. Schedules run on a regular basis from Florence with frequent trains between the five Cinque Terre villages. At last report, there is one taxi in town. Check with your lodging establishment for contact information. Keep in mind most places in town require going up and down hills. While somewhat difficult, the reward is a fantastic view of the sea and surrounding area.

Restaurants
Ripa Del Sole. Great food, with stunning sea views and excellent service. This restaurant is near the top of the hill for Riomaggiore, but worth the hike.

Address: Via De Gasperi, 4
http://www.ripadelsole.it/

Il Grottino. Located in the town center with a romantic environment. The seafood is amazing along with the wine. Reasonably priced.

Address: Via Colombo 237

Rio Bistrot. Located with a great view of the harbor; excellent pesto with a limited menu. It's not a huge place. Recommend call ahead for reservations.

Address: Via San Giacomo 10, 19017
Phone: 39-0187-920616

The best thing about Riomaggiore

The views and the distinct characteristics of the village. There is a beauty in the various town building colors, with each one seemingly leaning on the next. The view of the Mediterranean is mesmerizing, particularly at night when the moon reflects off the water.

Odds and Ends

It's uphill, and I mean uphill. But once you get to the top, you are rewarded with a view you won't soon forget. This area is also one of the best areas for picture-taking; undoubtedly many will print off and hang on your walls at home.

This is how Italian men get their reputation. We stopped at a church near the top of one of the villages. A gentleman was sitting on a bench in front of the church. He inquired if my wife wanted to sit next to him for a photo opportunity. She sat, then he asked for a kiss on the cheek, at which time he immediately turned and tried to kiss my wife on the lips. She turned as he kissed her on the cheek.

But I wonder: he asked my wife if she wanted to visit his wine cellar, but didn't invite me. Hmmm... Ya gotta love Italy.

Vernazza

The only natural port of the Cinque Terre, Vernazza remains car-free with hundreds of tourists visiting each day. It is a beautiful village with an equally beautiful harbor. Vernazza is a must see of the Cinque Terre.

Corniglia

The only village not adjacent to the sea, Corniglia rises above it and is surrounded by vineyards and terraces. A foot path leads the way to the village from the train station up the hill to a 377-step stairway. Corniglia itself is connected to the other villages via a foot path maintained by the park service. With a population of under 200, Corniglia is the least visited of the Cinque Terre.

There are some excellent restaurants in Corniglia including **Bar Terza Terra**. With an amazing view (and I mean amazing), food (try the bruschetta) and service, you won't be disappointed. This restaurant is worth the hike.

Address: Via Fieschi, 215, 19018
(+39) 0187-821411

Manarola

Often referenced as the oldest village of the Cinque Terre, Manarola features a vast array of colorful buildings. Although there isn't a beach, this community does offer the best deep-water swimming around. A ladder up the rocks and a shower are also provided for those willing to take the plunge. Manarola's primary occupations are fishing and wine-making.

There are a few excellent restaurants, one of my favorites being the **Nessun Dorma,** specializing in pesto and bruschetta, not to mention the great view over the sea. There is no fish on this menu. They feature cold meats, cheese, bread, and salad. The restaurant also offers a highly praised pesto class, a must if you love pesto as much as we do.

Monterosso di Mare

Reason to visit.

Great views of the water, beautiful and colorful buildings, easy to stroll around town, and a relaxing beach to sit and watch life go by. Monterosso is an easy stroll to the only beach in the area with a more active nightlife.

Background

In 1870 a railway was built to Monterosso di Mare, opening this ancient village to the world.

Separated into two distinct parts, Monterosso has an 'old' and 'new' town; a tunnel divides both sections. Frequently you will find street entertainers near the tunnel trying to earn a buck; and often very entertaining.

The beach at Monterosso runs along most of the coastline and is well used by tourists and locals. The only sand beach in the Cinque Terre where sunbathers come to lay out. In the summer months, Monterosso is often crowded with hundreds of tourists.

How to get there

By train. No other choice is reasonable although this is one of the few villages that is accessible by car, but not recommended due to the shortage of parking spaces.

Odds and Ends
Il Bazar, Monterosso
Neat little gift shop with some interesting items to purchase.

Restaurants
Enoteca da Eliseo
Cozy wine bar with great reviews.

Address: 3 Piazza Matteotti

Gastronomia San Martino
Highly rated restaurant with 'awesome pesto', featuring salads, seafood, and pasta.

Address: Via San Martino 3, 19016

Chapter 6
Venice and Nearby

Vaporetto (Vap oh ret toe)
Water Taxi

Featured in Italia! Magazine

Background

Located in the northeastern part of Italy, Venice is joined by a system of 117 bridges that link together the canals and the small islands. Visited by millions of tourists each year, the city itself has a population of around 55,000. During the Middle Ages and the Renaissance, Venice was recognized as the first international financial center.

When traveling to Venice by train, be sure and get off at the Venice Santa Lucia Station, not the Venice Mestre Station which is located on the mainland. You wouldn't be the first to make that mistake. As it is in a more industrial section of Venice, it is not exactly a tourist destination.

The beautiful buildings are built on closely spaced wooden piles and posts. Over the decades these wooden foundations have been slowly decaying, which is obviously a huge concern to the city and the world.

How to get there
Cars are not allowed in Venice. There are no roads. Trains do arrive on the island which most

often is the primary transportatio n to utilize. Cruise ships arrive daily, further crowding the city. The nearest airport is the Venice Marco Polo where you will take a combination of public buses and water bus (Vaporetto) from the airport.

Restaurants

Muro San Stae. Excellent seafood and pizza. Highly rated.

> Address: Campiello dello Spezier Santa Croce 2048
>
> Phone: 39 041 524 1628

Vino Vera. An excellent quiet place for wine and small bites; many locals come to this local watering hole. Vino Vera offers a local atmosphere with excellent service.

> Address: Fondamenta de la Misericordia Cannaregio 2497.

Sites to see

St. Mark's Square, also known as Piazza San Marco, is the principal public courtyard in Venice. The St. Mark church sits at the eastern side of the grand square. Along the sides you will find a couple of restaurants and shops. A couple of the restaurants will often have live music. Grab a table and chair, buy a glass of wine, and sit back and enjoy!

The churches throughout Italy are beautiful, there is no doubt. However, remember they are houses of worship. They are not tourist exhibits where one can freely roam around the altar or other sacred spaces. Show respect and dress appropriately.

Recommendations

After two days of sight-seeing, you may want to get away from the crowds and visit one of the outlying islands. You'll be glad you did. (See Burano and Torcello below). For restaurant recommendations, get off the beaten track to find many good restaurants. Don't be too afraid of getting lost, remember you are on an island. My recommendation is that if you have an exact location you are looking for, then there is no substitution for GPS service such as Google Maps. Venice roads are a confusing mish of circular and zig-zagging streets; they follow the canals and wind around the city creating a maze of confusing turns. I hate to admit it, but even with a map we still got lost for a few hours trying to locate a specific restaurant (which we never found!).

The best thing about Venice
The canals, the buildings, and the people are a photographer's dream. There is nothing more romantic, or picturesque than a photograph of the Venice canals, with the many boats and gondolas dotting the scene. One must also take a loved one on a gondola ride to complete the trip; there are an amazing number of gondolas available so be sure to check the price first. My recommendation is to stand back and observe the operators; some sing, some do not. Some will engage in conversation, while others obviously are just after the easy buck, or euro in this case.

Odds and Ends
On our last trip, we visited in April during a couple of wet, rainy days that descended upon Venice. We spent a good amount of time dodging and weaving amongst the thousands of tourist's umbrellas along the many crowded walkways, particularly those near the waterfront. Considering all the canals in Venice, that is pretty much the whole place.

Off the beaten path

Fondazione Querini Stampalia. An entrance-free library donated in 1869 by Count Giovanni Querini Stampalia, open Tuesdays through Saturday from 10:00 am until midnight, and Sundays and holidays from 10:00 am to 7:00 pm. This beautiful library contains thousands of volumes of books on various subjects in very nicely decorated rooms of oil paintings, ceiling frescos and Murano glass chandeliers. Even free Wi-fi is included. On the second floor, an impressive picture gallery of well-known artists is featured with a modest entrance fee required.

Address: Castello 4778, Campiello
Querini Stampalia - 30122 Venice

Tour. While in Venice, our guide, Elizaetta Amadi of toursbylocal.com gave us an outstanding tour, which she called the Venice bar-hopping; which was stopping for some local food or wine bars and tasting the samples(tapas) and the wine. Each of these local establishments we visited was outstanding:

Ai Schiavi a san Trovaso or Cantinone Già Schiavi

Address: Fondamenta Nani 992,
Dorsoduro - 30123
http://www.cantinaschiavi.com/

Cantina do Spade

Address: San Polo, 859, 30125

http://cantinadospade.com/en/

El Sbarlefo San Pantalon

Address: Dorsoduro 3757, 07041

http://www.elsbarlefo.it/

Tours in Venice – Contact: Elizabeth Amadi of toursbylocal.com (Guide 9517-110@toursbylocals.com)

Website: https://www.toursbylocals.com/Venicewithalocal

Want to see a wedding party in Venice? Pick a day. Any day.

North of Venice: Burano

The islands of Burano and Torcello are located north of Venice, about a forty (40) minute boat ride.

The current population of Burano is around 2800 with Burano most famous for its lace work and colored homes. If someone wishes to paint their home, they must first get the approval of the local government, who will grant permission based on colors that are permitted.

Background

Often rated among the ten most 'colorful' places in the world, Burano is associated with lacemaking as the primary tourist attraction. Additionally, Burano is known for its famous fish dishes, in this case, the 'risotto to go,' a fish broth in which the rice is cooked to a creamy texture and the fish is extracted from the "go," a common fish known from the Venice lagoon.

How to get there

The trip to Burano or Torcello requires a ride aboard the local boat transport, called a "vaporetto." These boats are the local water taxi and easy to board with comfortable seating. The trip itself takes about 40 minutes, depending on whether you decide to go to Torcello or Burano.

Recommendations

The best thing about Burano. There is no doubt about it, the colorful houses that exist in Burano.

Odds and Ends. While Torcello, a nearby island is a quick trip, Burano is a community that deserves a day's tour. The colorful buildings, lace making shops, and a tour of the town is a delightful experience.

Torcello

Located nearby on another island, Torcello is a lovely place to visit with only about 20 residents. It is the oldest continuously populated region of Venice and once held the largest population of the area, notably after the fall of the Roman Empire when thousands of people were escaping Attila the Hun as he swept through the Italian region.

Today you can easily access the island with the Vaporetti, walking the grounds and visiting the local church. The town has had many famous visitors including Princess Diana and years ago, and Ernest Hemingway, who spent a month here writing and hunting.

Restaurants

The small village also hosts three or four restaurants, notably Osteria Al Ponte del Diavolo and Locanda Cipriani, the latter opened by legendary Venetian Hotelier Giuseppe Cipriani in the 1940s. Locanda Cipriani reportedly a favorite by Mr. Hemmingway. Highly recommended by many who have stopped here.

Villa '600 Restaurant.

One of the best meals we experienced in Italy with a great relaxing atmosphere. We love this place and would most definitely return. Easy to locate, it is one of the first restaurants you will see on the left-hand side when entering the town.

It's a short walk to the town center from the dock. It is amazing that when you look at the history, this was the first and final stop for those escaping the fall of Rome; now it is an island of 20 residents. As Venice grew, Torcello declined.

The best thing about Torcello. It is a beautiful, quiet island. Earnest Hemingway visited here as did Princess Di.

We have seen very little police on the Italian highways. However, if you do see them standing on the side of the road with a miniature 'stop' sign and they point it at you, you had better stop...Radar speed traps do exist; you need to adhere to the speed limit. Otherwise, they will mail you a picture of the speeding violation to your rental car agency. This ticket will entail a monetary penalty plus a $75 administrative charge.

A not-very-nice surprise when you get home and see your VISA charge waiting for you in the mail box. I thought I would have 1 or 2 violation notices, but surprisingly nothing ever arrived... A strong recommendation: you need to rent a car to see the real Italy, much like visiting the U.S. The countryside is beautiful with mountain villages throughout the valleys, many you can't get to without a car. While driving a rental car may appear intimidating, think of it as going one kilometer (mile) at a time. Drive defensively, and you will survive.

The Lido

The Lido, or Venice Lido, is a seven-mile long sandbar island next to Venice, home to 20,000 residents and numerous hotels, restaurants, and shops. The well-known Venice Film Festival is held here every September. Bicycle riding around the island is easy and quite common. Access to the island is by Vaporetto (water bus) from Venice.

Many churches look rough on the outside but quite beautiful inside. It could easily be said that these churches cannot be replicated at any cost. The paintings, frescoes, stain glass, statues, architecture... all magnificent as you walk inside whatever church you visit. Do not underestimate the beauty of a church of even the smallest village you visit.

Tab A – Vacation Checklist

Vacation checklist	Comments
Determine dates of trip	
Make air reservations	*Check credit card points*
Reserve car if applicable	*Check out smaller villages for rental car locations (i.e. Alba)*
Obtain International driver's license	*Check AAA*
Arrange for transportation from the airport to hotel	*Taxi, train and or/bus service. Some hotels have transportation*
Make train reservations	*Usually, for long trips only- AAA can assist or direct*
Make lodging reservations	*Review TripAdvisor – Booking.com & AAA*
Ensure passports are current	
Purchase Money Belt	*AAA – travel stores*
Visit local travel stores	*(i.e. RickSteves, AAA)*
Determine luggage needs	*"The less, the better"; Purchase TSA lock*
Review medical insurance	
Review car insurance needs if applicable	*Use reputable company- review complaints online*
Notify credit card companies	*They will suspend the use if not notified*
Contact cell phone company	*Review overseas program options*
Review Skype computer use if desired	
Obtain international calling procedures to the U.S. from Italy	
Learn basic Italian words	*Many phone apps can assist*
Bring good quality camera	*Cell phones do take excellent pictures*
Utilize social media if desired (i.e. Facebook)	*Daily updates for friends and family*

Good quality walking shoes	*The cobblestone streets will kill your feet!*
Light raincoat	*Purchase inexpensive umbrella in Italy if needed*
Bring laptop or tablet if desired	*Be aware of thieves especially in crowded areas*
Bring electric converter	*Hairdryers not converted will blow circuits!*
Understand emergency overseas medical procedures	*Contact your insurance company for information*

Tab B – Recommendation Lodgings

No matter where you plan to spend the night, there is no shortage of lodging choices in Italy. There are many great places to stay and just as many not-so-great. When choosing a room, be sure to check out the reviews; also check out the amenities. Will you require air conditioning? Private bath? Single bed or double? The costs vary, and you will be surprised at the number of choices under $100 a night. Also, check out the payment system, will it be cash, credit card or bank transfer? The following have all received top reviews, several I have stayed at with no complaints whatsoever.

Lodging pictures are from the respective websites unless otherwise noted.

Rome

"A View of Rome" bed and breakfast.

Centrally located close to the Vatican. Great location, view and price.

Address: Piazza del Risorgimento n.14 - Floor 4 - Int. 11 - 00192 Rome
Telephone: (+39) 06.39737845
http://www.bbaviewofrome.it/en/
Email: info@bbaviewofrome.it

Hotel Santa Maria

While in Rome, one of our favorite hotels is the Hotel Santa Maria, located in the Trastevere neighborhood of Rome. This small hotel is in the vibrant area of Rome, particularly at night when tourists and locals alike come out to the local restaurants and nightlife. But one thing Rome does not have a shortage of is reasonably priced accommodations to fit any budget, whether small or large.

Suggestion

> If there is an alley, there is an outdoor café. Just an ugly alley in the morning, turns into a vibrant community from 11 am to after midnight. Be sure to visit the Trastevere district in Rome, popular with the locals and tourists alike.

When leaving this hotel for the day or night, be sure to mark on your map where the hotel is located. While it is somewhat centrally located in this great part of Rome, the streets curl, snake, and twist in many directions. We found ourselves going in circles before we discovered our way back.

Website: "Awarded the Certificate of Excellence and ranked in the top 10 hotels in Rome by TripAdvisor, the Hotel Santa Maria Rome is a superior 3-star hotel situated in the charming district of Trastevere. Consistently rated by guests as a fantastic hotel which offers excellent value for money, the Hotel Santa Maria is situated in a completely renovated 16th Century cloister offering 19 comfortable rooms and positioned within walking distance of the major archaeological & tourist sites of Rome."

Address: Vicolo del Piede, 2
Telephone: +39 06 5894626
http://hotelsantamariatrastevere.it/#popup1
Email: info@hotelsantamaria.info

Hotel Savoy Roma

Centrally located, this luxury 120 room hotel has spectacular 360-degree views of Rome from the rooftop garden and restaurant. It would be hard to beat the view, the restaurant, and the hotel rooms.

Address: Via Ludovisi, 15 Roma 00187
Telephone +39 06421.551
http://www.savoy.it/eng/4_star_rome_h
otels.htm
Email: reservations@savoy.it

Portrait Roma

This five-star boutique hotel is located close to the Spanish Steps on a quiet side street, close to shopping and other historic sites. Rooms are quite comfortable with kitchenettes and a friendly staff that is consistently rated as the best with hospitality. Breakfast is served on the roof terrace. One of the top rated hotels in Rome.

Address: Via Bocca di Leone, 23, 00187
Telephone: (+39) 06 69380742
https://www.lungarnocollection.com/por trait-roma
Email:
reservations@lungarnocollection.com

Trastevere's Friends Lodging
Highly rated by several websites this lodging has six air-conditioned rooms with kitchens. 18-inch flat screen televisions in each room with

complimentary wireless. Housekeeping provided daily. Trastevere's Friends is located in the popular tourist area of Trastevere.

Address: Via Benedetto Musolino 23
Trastevere 00153 Rome
Telephone: (+39) 06 9357 7587
http://www.bnbromatrastevere.it/en/contact/
Email: trasteveresfriends@gmail.com

Hotel Castle

Located at the edge of Rome, this is one of our favorite hotels to stay at based on the service we have experienced. Although not within walking distance to central Rome, the hotel offers car service at no charge to the local train station where you can take a quick ride to the center of Rome. When you get back to the train station, call for a fast return to the hotel. On our last stay, we did not have our cell phone with us; they were kind enough to loan us their cell phone so could call when ready. What service! The rooms are also spotless, spacious and very economical.

> Address: Salita di Castel Giubileo 196, 00138
> Telephone: 06 8804084
> Website: http://www.hotelcastle.it/en/
> E-mail: info@hotelcastle.it

Appia Antica Resort

This boutique apart-hotel stands four miles away from the Coliseum, surrounded by one of the most beautiful places in Rome and, maybe, of the world: The Archeological Park of the Appian Way. An area almost in the center of the town, but surrounded by the countryside, where herds of sheep stay beside the ruins. The hosts will assist in giving you directions and suggestions to discover this place, as well as hidden hotspots of the city center. Tours can be arranged, no matter what or where, from the peaceful experience of the breath-taking Appian Way, up to a near-death experience darting amongst the cars of Rome with a tour guide on Vespa scooter (I probably go for the first one, if you don't mind!). A special occasion? They will arrange a bottle of champagne or flowers upon your request. Cooking classes can also be organized with famous Italian chefs, along with babysitting services or workshops for your children. Here you will find not simple rooms, but reasonably-priced apartments of different sizes, embraced by a beautiful enclosed garden.

Address: Via Appia Pignatelli, 368
Telephone: (+39) 0(6) 45 44 80 35
http://www.appiaanticaresort.com/
Email: info@appiaanticaresort.com

Roof Suite Rome Historic Residence

Close to the Roman Forum, city walks and other historical sites, this centrally located bed and breakfast resides in the Monti neighborhood of Rome. Every room has air conditioning, flat screen TV, coffee machine and a private bathroom. Slippers and bathrobes are also included! There is a shared lounge at the lodging. Car rental service is also available.

The bed and breakfast lodging also host a highly-rated rooftop restaurant.

Address: Via Palermo 36, Rione Monti, 00184
Telephone: (+39) 06 487 0919
http://www.roofsuiterome.com/en/
info@roofsuiterome.com

Hotel Artemide

A 4-star hotel that prides itself on hospitality, this hotel is centrally located on Via Nazionale, one of the most vibrant streets in the city. If you desire top restaurants, historic sites, shopping, art galleries, theatres or bars, all are located within walking distance. The hotel services include a top-rated restaurant and an impressive spa offering massages along with a hot tub, Turkish bath, Finnish spa, ice cascade and a relation room. The luxury romantic rooms or suites are each different in layout and size and add to the uniqueness of this hotel. Each room hosts a smart TV with a free mini-bar to snack or to engage with a drink at the end of the day. A dome of art Nouveau style in the lobby welcomes you in this completely restored magnificent building dating from 1877.

Address: Via Nazionale, 22 - 00184
Telephone: (+39) 06.489911
http://www.hotelartemide.it/en/
Email: info@hotelartemide.it

Orvieto
Antica Olivaia Agriturismo, Orvieto.
Located about 15 minutes outside of town, reasonable prices, nice, quiet rooms in a rural setting.

From their website: "This quaint bed and breakfast in Orvieto is located only fifteen minutes from the main "autostrada" or highway which connects Florence to Rome. From this base, a myriad of medieval towns and enchanting villages are located within easy reach including Civita di Bagnoregio, Bolsena, Todi, Città della Pieve, Montefalco, Spoleto, Perugia, Assisi, and Montepulciano."

Beautiful scenery, peaceful, a gorgeous swimming pool, 700 tree olive grove, great food, and hospitality; they also produce top-notch extra virgin olive oil. The wife is formerly of Chicago and speaks fluent Italian; her husband is Italian and quite a chef. They offer dinner at night for a fee; well worth the money.

Address: San Bartolomeo, 17 - Orvieto (TR)
Telephone: (+39) 0763 215262 - (+39) 334 1850112
Website: www.anticaolivaia.com Civita
Email: info@anticaolivaia.com

Civita di Bagnoregio

When staying in local, older lodging facilities, one must remember that these places are not always sound proof. There is nothing like trying to eat breakfast while an amorous couple is wildly and loudly "doing it" with the noise echoing throughout the kitchen. During breakfast, the hostess was quite embarrassed and often apologizing while my wife comically quipped "I will have what they are having!"

B&B Sant'Angelo 42, Orvieto

Located in the center of Orvieto, this bed and breakfast is a great location to visit the city if you are without a rental car.

The B&B offers three bedrooms, very clean and quiet; you wouldn't know you were in the center of town. Breakfasts are the typical Italian fare with friendly hosts. Somehow, on our last trip, we managed, to get on the wrong train that resulted in our arrival around midnight. The owner was gracious enough to ensure someone was on site upon our arrival. Another justification to carry a cell phone in case of an emergency or missed transport.

> Address: Via Sant'Angelo, 42 - Orvieto (TR) 05018
> Telephone: (+39) 348 7757136
> http://www.bborvieto.com/
> Email: info@bborvieto.com

The B&B, located in the center of Orvieto, was a great location to explore the beautiful village by foot especially in the early morning when the tourists have not yet arrived and the town is just waking up. Orvieto is very clean with no graffiti on any of the buildings and great restaurants for food, although I caution that if you find a restaurant serving an American breakfast omelet, you may want to skip it. They appear to think Americans love salt and lots of it.

B&B Valentina
Sound proof and recently remodeled, this B&B features private bathrooms, showers, hairdryers and choice of double or triple beds. Very reasonably priced and located near the town's historic center, this B&B comes highly rated by previous guests. For those desiring a country

setting, the owner has apartments for rent just ten minutes from town.

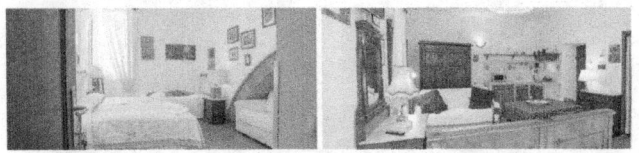

Address: Via Vivaria 7, 05018
Telephone: 00 390763341607
www.bandbvalentina.com
Email: camerevalentina@gmail.com

The Hotel Duomo
Centrally located in Orvieto, this 3-star, 18-room hotel is close to the Duomo and the Piazza. Rooms are clean and comfortable with the typical Italian fare for the buffet breakfast.

Address: Vicolo Maurizio 7 -05018 Orvieto
Telephone: (+39) 0763 341887
www.orvietohotelduomo.com
Email: info@orvietohotelduomo.com

Casa Sogno
Centrally located only 2000 feet from the Duomo and the nearby opera, Attico Blu and Chalet Medioevale, both 2-unit apartment buildings, have private bathrooms with shower or tub, plus a sitting area, dining room and

kitchen with dishwasher. The units are two bedrooms each. A flat screen TV is also on hand for those whose walking legs have given out. The hosts have an outstanding reputation for service with extremely clean apartments. Parking is available.

Attico Blu

The owner also has a one-bedroom unit overlooking the Tirreno sea in Tuscany on the same website.

Casa
Secchio

Address: Attico Blu: Vicolo Angelo Da Orvieto 2 - 05018 Orvieto (TR)
Chalet Medioevale: Vicolo Santo Stefano 2, 05018 Orvieto (TR)
www.casasogno.com
Email: case.orvieto@gmail.com

Altarocca Wine Resort

Located on thirty acres of vineyards and olive groves outside Orvieto, this resort meets the needs for those seeking luxury lodging.

Three swimming pools, bocce ball court, free Wi-Fi, bicycles, wellness and spa, top-rated restaurant, cooking seminars and winery, this resort has it all. The lodging itself consists of 4 villas with suites and apartments. Prices are surprisingly affordable for this type of luxury.

Address: Rocca Ripesena, 62 - 05010
Telephone: (+39) 0763 344210 / 393437
http://www.altaroccawineresort.com/en/
Email: info@altaroccawineresort.com

Cinque Terre

Monterosso is a beautiful village with easy walking along the city streets. This is one of the few villages of the Cinque Terre you can drive and park.

Hotel Pasquale, Monterosso

Very reasonably priced, great views of the waters with excellent and friendly service and breakfast. The hotel hosts fifteen (15) rooms most with great views of the water. They go out of their way to ensure you are satisfied with your accommodations. We have stayed here before and will most definitely stay again.

Tip: When looking for the hotel building signage, instead look for the sandwich sign. It's on the sidewalk in front of you!

Address: Via Fegina, 4 - 19016 Monterosso al Mare (SP) - Cinque Terre – Italy
Telephone: (+39) 0187.817477 /817550
http://www.hotelpasquale.it/
Email: pasquale@pasini.com

"I Limoni Di Thule", Riomaggiore

Beautiful apartment setting with a fantastic view of the water, especially at night when you can watch the fishermen catch anchovies. Watch as their boat lights slowly come together while they gather the nets. We have stayed here twice and hoped to do so again. The owners are super with hospitality with the wife speaking fluent English.

Suggestion: Be sure and get clear directions to this lodging. It can be a little tricky the very first time and fortunately the owner Christina was out looking for us (and found us!). Another example of her hospitality.

Address: Via Tracastello 44 19017 Riomaggiore
Telephone: +0039 349 62 49 505
Christina O'Brien
www.limonicamere.it
Email: info@limonicamere.it

Manarola is often recognized as the most colorful of the villages of the Cinque Terre.

La Torretta, Manarola

Situated in an ancient tower in the center of town with stunning views of the bay, the rooms of this lodge overlook the views of the vineyard on one side or the blue waters of the Mediterranean on the other. Soundproof windows, security doors, equipped kitchen, Wi-Fi, television, coffee machine, beach towels, safe box and only a five-minute walk from the train station, La Torretta is a perfect central location for exploring Cinque Terre.

Address: Vicolo Volto 20 | Piazza della Chiesa, 19017 Manarola, Italy
Telephone: (+39) 0187 920327
www.torrettas.com
Email: torretta@cdh.it

Bed and Breakfast, Il Giardino Incantato,
Monterosso La Torretta (Manarola)

From the website: *"A relaxing holiday where the refined details blend with a sophisticated atmosphere according to the tradition and comfort. We'll take care of you in a 16th Century House, with a typically Ligurian garden, where you can relax and enjoy our excellent breakfasts."*

Located in the old town of Monterosso with just a one-minute walk to the beach, the B&B hosts four double rooms each with a private bathroom.

Great reviews posted from previous guests with reasonable rates for accommodations.

> Address: via Mazzini, 18
> Telephone: (+39) 0187.818315
> Telephone: (+39) 333.2649252
> http://www.ilgiardinoincantato.net/
> Email: giardino_incantato@libero.it

B&B SoleMare, Monterosso

Located 10-15 minutes from the train station in the very center of the historic section of Monterosso al Mare, minutes away from small shops and the beach, this B&B has two quiet double rooms with private bathrooms. SoleMare additionally has a rooftop terrace with great views of the town, sea and nearby mountains. SoleMare is reasonably priced with great

reviews. The owner speaks English as well as Swedish, Italian and Polish.

Address: Via S Martino 11
Telephone: 0039 3290793865 Wanda Ternström

http://www.bedandbreakfastsolemarecin
queterre.com/index/
Email: wate99@gmail.com

Hotel Stella della Marina, Monterosso
Located in the old town, this 10-room hotel is minutes away from the beach and the train station. Built in the 17th century, the floors 2 through 5 have no elevator. The rooms are air-conditioned with private bathrooms, something that is not always found in Italy. Satellite TV and Internet Wi-Fi are also offered.

Address: Via XX Settembre 11 - 19016
Monterosso al mare
Telephone: 0187.802669
http://www.stelladellamarina.com/en-
hotel.php
Email: info@stelladellamarina.com

Hotel Marina, Monterosso

Located in a quiet area, 100 meters from the sea, this beautiful 25 room hotel offers private bathrooms, air-conditioning, Wi-Fi, safe and mini-bar. This hotel has an elevator, restaurant, reading room and a big buffet for breakfast. From May to October breakfast is served outside in the garden of lemons.

Via Buranco 40, 19016 Monterosso al Mare
Telephone: (+39) 0187-817613
http://www.hotelmarina5terre.com/
Email: marina@hotelmarina5terre.com

Camere Giuliano – Vernazza

This bed and breakfast is situated in the center of Vernazza with a breathtaking view of the sea. Conveniently located close to the train station, the lodging host is extremely dedicated toward service to the customer. The roof top patio is another positive aspect to this B&B.

Address: Localita Capanna 1, 19018
Telephone: 0039 333 341 4792
http://www.cameregiuliano.com/english
/information.html
Email: giuliano@cdh.it

Levanto

Don't want to fight the crowds in Cinque Terre, but still want to visit? Try Levanto, a short five-minute reliable train ride from Monterosso. Quite popular with tourists, this village has many picturesque historic buildings as well as a relaxing beach. Levanto, meaning 'place of the rising sun' has been existence since the Roman times. The train station stops near the town center, making it easy to arrive at your lodging destination. During high tourist season, the town center is closed to traffic.

Hotel Carla
This hotel, located near the town center and the train station, has been in operation since 1960 and has been nicely remodeled since then. Hotel services include free Wi-Fi, air conditioning, tourist information, restaurant, bar, and a reading room. Hotel services can even arrange

for a tour of the town or at the beach. The rooms are quite elegant, many with balconies.

Address: Via Martiri della Liberta' 28, 19015
Telephone (+39) (0)187 80.82.75
http://www.carlahotel.com/en/Home
Email: info@carlahotel.com

Park Hotel Argento

Quite beautiful and recently constructed, this hotel hosts seven suites and 40 double rooms. Conveniently located near the coast, the hotel has a swimming pool with a massage station, a wellness center with sauna, Turkish bath and an 'emotional' shower (although for the life of me I have no idea what that is). Outdoor parking is available for free, and a parking garage is available for a fee. Air conditioning, satellite television, safe deposit box, and the Internet are provided. Outstanding restaurant on site with local and international cuisine.

Address: Via Sant'Anna s.n. 19015 (SP) Liguria
Telephone: (+39) 0187 801223
https://www.parkhotelargento.com/en/index.php
Email: info@parkhotelargento.com

Bonassola

Located on the Ligurian coast between Levanto and Monterosso, Bonassola offers tourists a choice of a quieter village to vacation with long sandy beaches where you can rent chairs and umbrellas. This tiny village is quite charming with cozy coffee shops and bars. From Levanto, it is a two-minute train ride or an hour walk along the hiking trail. It was only in 2010 that the tunnels leading from Levanto to Bonassola were restored. The result was a great walking or bike trail with scenic views.

Hotel delle Rose

Recently refurbished, this 25-room hotel hosts orthopedic mattresses, air-conditioning, mini-bar, satellite television, free Wi-Fi and quiet rooms. A restaurant is on site, with the possibility to visit the kitchen and witness the food preparation upon request. The highlight of the hotel is the roof garden overlooking the incredible views of the sea and the nearby hills. Prices are quite reasonable.

Address: Via Giuseppe Garibaldi, 8, 19011
Bonassola
Telephone: (+39) 0187 813713
http://www.hoteldellerosebonassola.it/en
Email: info@hoteldellerosebonassola.it

Venice

There is no shortage of hotels and bed and breakfasts throughout Venice; it just depends on your budget and desires. But realize those most desirable go fast; research and book early.

Al Ponte Antico Hotel

Very popular with visiting guests, this small, 4-star hotel sits on the Grand Canal with a great view of the Rialto Bridge. A former palace dating back to the 1500s, this hotel was recently meticulously remodeled ensuring to preserve the style and charm of a Venetian residence.

Address: Calle dell'Aseo, Cannaregio 5768
- 30131
Telephone: (+39) 041-2411944
www.alponteantico.com
Email: info@alponteantico.com

Gio' and Gio' Bed and Breakfast

Lovely B&B located in the center of Venice, off one of the canals (aren't they all canals?!!). Very reasonably priced and quiet.

Address: Calle de le Ostreghe San Marco
2439
30124 - Venezia
Telephone: (+39) 347-3665016
www.giogiovenice.com
Email: info@giogiovenice.com

'You and Me' Bed and Breakfast, Venice

Located in the heart of the Venice historical center with proximity to the Rialto Bridge and its famous market. Saint Mark square is a short walk as is the water transport. The lodging features three rooms with beams showing to add a historical flavor. There is a common area where breakfast is served. The rooms feature satellite television, Internet service, air conditioning and heating. Prices are quite reasonable.

Address: S.Polo, 1459/A – Calle de la Madoneta – 30125 Venezia
Telephone: (+39) 0415226507 – Mobile: (+39) 3465768385
http://bbyouandme.com/index_en.html
Email: info@bbyouandme.com

Agriturismo La Barena

A six-bedroom, 2-flat bed and breakfast situated mid-point of the lagoon north of Venice. A relaxing escape from the rat race of life in an area without new modern development and with a small dirt road to access it. The units are situated in the farmhouse on the property and can be combined into apartments if so desired.

A quality restaurant is on site as well. The restaurant specializes in local fish and meat dishes using local produce whenever possible.

Bike rental is available as well as a canoe that can be provided to transverse the local ponds featuring local birds and flamingos; a boat hire can be used to visit the nearby islands of Torcello, Burano San Francesco del Deserto.

The room rate is extremely reasonable at 30/60 euro per person per night (Depending on seasonality), at the time of this book printing. The pictures alone motivate you toward reserving this place for your next vacation.

The nearby seaside community of Jesolo (or Iesolo) is a resort destination with over 4 million visitors a year.

> Address: via Lio Maggiore, 21, 30016 Jesolo
> Telephone: (+39) 348 3681314
> http://agriturismo-labarena.it/
> Email: info@agriturismo-labarena.it

Villa Mocenigo

This villa hosts ten rooms in the Venetian style with bathrooms and air conditioning provided. Satellite TV, Wi-Fi, shower, and towels are provided. All rooms are spacious, well-lit and recently remodeled.

The farm is based in Mirano on five acres of seasonal crops with pigs, goats, geese, ducks, chickens, and hens populating the farm.

Villa Mocenigo has a restaurant on-site offering popular and typical Venetian meals.

Address: Via Viasana, 59, 30035 Mirano VE
Phone: (+39) 338 3629268
http://www.villamocenigo.com/index.ph p/it/
Email: info@villamocenigo.com

Tab C – Top Festivals

Italy is famous for its food, cultural and wine festivals. The below list is not a complete list, in fact, Italy may have enough festivals to write a book on just that subject alone. But it can give you an idea of the type and number of events Italy offers for the visiting tourist. For more information consult your computer search engine for specific dates and events.

January
> New Year's Day is a national holiday, probably because of the amount of alcohol consumed the night before.

February

> Carnevale, Ivrea, located in the Piedmont Region. Okay, not quite Cinque Terre, but here they have the annual parade followed by an orange-throwing battle in the center of town. Wearing a red hat means you are not one of the throwers but doesn't prevent you from getting hit.

> "Carnevale di Venezia," Venice, Italy. One of the most well-known festivals in the world. Buy a mask and rent a costume, then head over to a ball.

March

La Spezia street market featuring over 600 vendors. La Spezia is a short 8-minute train ride from Cinque Terre.

Saint Patrick's Day, mid-March. Yes, it is celebrated here in hundreds of bars across the country.

March 15th each year, Commemoration of Caesar's death. Over 2000 years since Italy's most famous ruler was assassinated, this event is still marked annually in Rome.

April

Vinitaly. Verona, Italy. Wine festival – one of the biggest wine shows you will ever attend. This event brings in thousands of visitors with over 4000 exhibitors showing off their wines.

Rome City Birthday Celebration, April 21st. Fireworks and parades. Other highlights include a trench-digging ritual (Tracciato del solco) and a parade of 2000 people in traditional Roman attire.

Liberation Day- nationwide, April 25. This day celebrates the liberation from the Nazi occupation at the end of the Second World War and the fall of Benito Mussolini.

Festival of St. Mark's Day, April 25th, Venice. Venetians celebrate their patron saint each year with a Mass, then follow with live music and a boat race.

April to October every year. Opera season held at the Vernazza town hall every Wednesday and Friday (Cinque Terre).

Easter Sunday, throughout Italy. Most high-end street shops will be closed, but museums and art galleries will be open.

May

Early May. The Snake Handlers Procession. Cocullo. Enough said.

La Palombella Pentecost Sunday celebration, Orvieto. Traditional festival with fireworks in the evening.
Feast of Corpus Domini. Orvieto. A costumed procession with the streets decorated with flowers.

Vogalonga Regatta, Venice. 2100 boats and 8000 rowers turn the Venice canals into the world's largest regatta

Feast of Corpus Domini – Monterosso and Vernazza. Procession on a carpet of flowers.

Feast of the Ascension, late May. Venice. Annual religious festival. The highlight each year as the mayor leads an impressive flotilla across the lagoon where he'll toss a ring under the waves to symbolize the city's bond with the sea.

Lemon Festival in Monterosso al Mare, Cinque Terre. Residents celebrate with the most common fruit in the Cinque Terre with awards going to the largest lemon. Live music surrounds the streets of Monterosso.

Cantine Aperte, the last Sunday in May each year, means 'open cellars' and is the one day a year when over 800 wineries open their doors for wine-tasting. http://www.movimentoturismovino.it/en/home/

June

The Festa della Repubblica, also known as Republic Day, is a national holiday celebrated on June 2 throughout Italy with Rome hosting the largest festival.

The Feast of Corpus Christi or Corpus Domini is celebrated 60 days after Easter around June 24 in various parts of Italy. In Orvieto, a celebration is held with flowers decorating the streets and over 400 people in a costumed procession.

Corniglia of Cinque Terre, a large traditional cake "Torta dei Fieschi" is made on June 29th, the day of San Pietro and Paolo. All participants get to sample a small piece of the cake.

San Giovanni Festival, Riomaggiore. Held in late June.

MORE Festival, Venice. Around the second week in June a city-wide program of music, light shows, and art exhibits.

July

Mid-July. The Redentore (The Redeemer) Church Feast Day is held on the third Sunday on Venice's Giudecca Island. Tourists will find a parade of decorated boats, concerts, and fireworks display show.

Roman neighborhood of Trastevere, the last two weeks of July hosts a neighborhood street fair.

At the foot of the Spanish Steps is held the international fashion show, Donne Sotte Le Stelle, in late July.

July to mid-August. One of two times during the year where Rome hosts huge summer sales (saldi) in particularly with clothing.

Late July in Levanto. The city celebrates the day of San Giacomo and the celebration of the sea. The two-day festival's highlight involves large crosses that are carried along the main street of the city.

August

In early August, Manarola of Cinque Terre celebrates the day of San Lorenzo with a procession and a blessing of the sea. Several artists arrive to paint in the villages and on the hiking trails.

Early August. Mare Mosso festival in Bonassola, near Cinque Terre. Week celebration of children and the theater.

Six theater companies for young people will present daily shows, free to the public.

Mid-August.   August 15, Ferragosto (Assumption Day), a national holiday where many shops and businesses will be closed. Celebrations include food, wine, and fireworks in various communities throughout Italy although many Italians take the day to head toward the beaches.

September

On the second weekend of September, the Anchovy festival is held in Monterosso.

Venice film festival in early September.

Venice's Regatta Storica historic boat race takes place the first Sunday in September. In nearby Burano island, Burano Regatta boat race is celebrated the third weekend in September.

Juliet's birthday (Romeo and Juliet) is celebrated September 12th in Verona.

October

Rome Film Festival held in mid-October for about ten days. Buy your tickets before they sell out.
www.romacinemafest.it

Truffle festival, Alba. One of the largest truffle festivals in the world, it may be worth a stop if you are taking a train from Cinque Terre to Venice. Festival includes food, music, exhibits, wine tasting, amusement rides and more.
www.fieradeltartufo.org

Venice marathon, late October. For those willing and able to run a fast, quick course. www.venicemarathon.it

International Accordion Festival, mid-October in Castelfidardo, a village in Marche. Close to Rome? Nope, I just had to enter that because I didn't know they had festivals for accordions.

November

November 1, All Saints Day is a national holiday, so many of the shops you wish to visit will be closed; most tourist attractions and museums will remain open.

Rome Jazz festival, most of November. Held at the Auditorium Parco della Musica.

November 22. Rome. Feast of Saint Cecilia. Celebrated at Santa Cecilia in Trastevere.

December

Rome is one of the most popular destinations for the Christmas holiday. Some of the best shopping deals are found at the Christmas markets, many of the markets open around December 13, Santa Lucia Day. In Rome, Piazza Navona holds a big Christmas market.

Nativity pageants take place December 24-26 in various areas of Italy.

Manarola of the Cinque Terre is host to a huge nativity scene on the hillside overlooking the city.

Huge after-Christmas sales in Rome that will last until mid-February.

New Year's Eve is known as La Festa di San Silvestro, where fireworks, music, and dancing often extend to sunrise where partiers can welcome the first morning of the new year with the festivals often accompanied by quite a good amount of great food.

Tab D – Key Internet Addresses and Tours

	Internet address	**Comments**
Italia! Magazine	http://www.italytravelandlife.com/	Beautiful and well-written magazine of Italy
Tripadvisor.com	www.tripadvisor.com	Check reviews and prices for lodging and restaurants along with things to do
Agriturismo.it	www.agriturismo.it	Great Italian website on working farm lodgings throughout Italy.
Booking.com	www.booking.com	Another great site to check for lodging and restaurants.
Train travel	www.Raileurope.com www.Italiarail.com	Train travel throughout Italy
AAA	www.aaa.com	Travel expertise, products, and international driver's license

Tours

Toursbylocal.com	www.toursbylocal.com	Many local tour guides for many cities at reasonable rates
Venice-Toursbylocal.com	guide 9517-110@toursbylocals.com	Highly rated Venice tour by guide Elisabetta Amadi
Marco's Way Day Tours	http://www.marcosway.it/links.php Phone: (+39) 328 7644 253 email: info@marcosway.it	Le Marche region (South of Venice). 5 Star rating TripAdvisor
Viator Tours	www.Viator.com	Italian tours, notably around Rome.
Eternity Tours	www.througheternity.com	Tours in Rome and other locations
Dark Rome Tours	www.citywonders.com or www.darkrome.com	Tours of Rome and other venues
Rick Steves	www.ricksteves.com	Notable travel expert offering advice and tours
Citalia	www.citalia.com	Personalized tours with over 85 years of experience
Perillo Tours	www.perillotours.com	Decades of tour experience throughout Italy

INDEX

About the Author
Steven Craig

 Steven Craig has recorded and photographed his experiences highlighting the history and his humorous 'misadventures' while traveling throughout the country of Italy. His book also provides pre-trip recommendations for how to prepare and once in Italy, offers recommendations on lodging, travel, food, and wine.

Steven's intent to readers is to provide vital information that will assist in the traveler's preparation and vacation to Italy, particularly to those visitors unfamiliar with traveling overseas. While no trip is perfect, Steven shows the humorous side of traveling abroad, all a part of fully enjoying the total experience of traveling and visiting new lands.

This pocket-size book can be easily carried for reference to the fascinating communities of Rome, Venice, and the beautiful Cinque Terre. If you are looking for quick facts, or recommendations for top lodging, restaurants or even tours, this book delivers.

Comments and recommendations may be sent to SCraig7002@gmail.com

"Informative, comprehensive, and great resource for anyone planning a trip to Italy. Steve shares his wealth of knowledge and provides superb tips in this essential must-have guide."

Rob Espinosa
Honolulu, HI

Updates to this guidebook may be found at www.italytravelandadventures.com

ISBN-13: 978-1546671886
ISBN-10: 1546671889

Made in the USA
Monee, IL
07 July 2026

56544411R10105